Library Assessment in Higher Education

Library Assessment in Higher Education

Joseph R. Matthews

A Member of the Greenwood Publishing Group

Westport, Connecticut • London

Library of Congress Cataloging-in-Publication Data

Matthews, Joseph R.
  Library assessment in higher education / Joseph R. Matthews.
  p. cm.
  Includes bibliographical references and index.
  ISBN-13: 978–1–59158–531–2 (alk. paper)
  1. Academic libraries—Evaluation. 2. Libraries and colleges. 3.
  Educational evaluation. I. Title.
  Z675.U5M354 2007
  027.7—dc22   2007018690

British Library Cataloguing in Publication Data is available.

Library of Congress Catalog Card Number: 2007018690
ISBN-13: 978-1-59158-531-2

First published in 2007

Libraries Unlimited, 88 Post Road West, Westport, CT 06881
A Member of the Greenwood Publishing Group, Inc.
www.lu.com

Printed in the United States of America

The paper used in this book complies with the
Permanent Paper Standard issued by the National
Information Standards Organization (Z39.48–1984).

10 9 8 7 6 5 4 3 2 1

Contents

Acknowledgments

Library Assessment in Higher Education is much improved by the careful and thoughtful review and reflection provided by a number of individuals. My deep thanks and appreciation go to Mary M. Somerville, Associate Dean of the Dr. Martin Luther King Jr. Library at San Jose State University; Charles McClure, Francis Eppes Professor and Director, Information Use Management and Policy Institute, Florida State University; Rachel Applegate, Assistant Professor, Indiana University School of Library and Information Science; and Karen Neurohr, Assessment Librarian, Oklahoma State University, who made extensive suggestions and comments.

Steve Hiller, Director of Assessment and Planning, University of Washington libraries; Amos Lakos, Librarian, Rosenfeld Management Library at the University of California Los Angeles; James Nalen, Planning, Assessment & Organizational Development Coordinator at George Mason University; Bob Molyneux, Chief Statistician for Sirsi/Dynix; Jim Self, Director of Management Information Services at the University of Virginia library; Mark Thompson, Assistant Library Director, of the Bergen Community College in Paramus, New Jersey; J. Stephen Town, Director of Knowledge Services, Cranfield University; and Professor Larry White, who teaches at the Department of Library Science & Instructional Technology, College of Education, East Carolina University, also provided helpful comments.

I am indebted to all these individuals for their suggestions, which improved the book considerably. However, any errors or lack of clarity in the information presented in this book are obviously my responsibility, not theirs.

I am also appreciative of the many libraries that provided articles and other materials. In addition, I would be negligent to not mention the outstanding service provided by Teri Roundenbush, head of the Interlibrary Loan/Resource Sharing unit, and her dedicated staff at the California State University San Marcos library. Her cheerful attitude and a commitment to excellence are a constant reminder of what quality service is in a library.

I must also acknowledge the encouragement and support of Sue Easun and Ron Maas at Libraries Unlimited. In addition, I do appreciate the wonderful job of copyediting performed by Sharon DeJohn. As always, Sharon is a delight to work with and has made the text of this book so much more readable.

Chapter

1

Introduction

Given the events of the past decade, academic librarians perhaps know better than anyone else that the institutions they manage—and their own roles—may face extinction over the next decade.—Jerry Campbell[1]

The intention of this book is to explain and clarify the practice of assessment at academic institutions, so that a library manager can assess library services as the first step in beginning to understand the impact of the library on student learning outcomes and research productivity.

Determining the outcomes of an academic library within the context of its college or university environment is challenging. First is the question of assessment focus, which must be linked to assessment intentions. An assessment may focus on the individuals who utilize the library's collection (physical and electronic) and its services—both face-to-face and technology-mediated or virtual. A broader perspective would attempt to identify the collective impacts of all the library's services and systems on all of the library's present and potential customers—that is, to gauge the contribution of the library to the total educational experience of its students, faculty, and researchers.

Similarly, methodological research choices will affect the generalizability of the assessment results. So the "anchoring" question is: What is the purpose of the investigation? Is the goal to describe the influence of an academic library on the life of an individual, or is it to characterize the impact on a specific set of customers or population served? Or does the study strive—in a more grandiose fashion—to reveal the impact of library services and systems on the higher education mission of campus research, teaching, and learning? These questions have significant bearing on the assessment design and analysis. In addition, intention has considerable bearing on decisions about dissemination of findings.

The purpose of this book is to provide a broad perspective about assessment activities that occur in colleges and universities as a preface to exploring library assessment and evaluation options aimed at determining the library's contribution to the "holistic" success of an academic organization's mission and vision.

1

The role, purpose, and value of academic library assessment must be "anchored" in an organization's purpose. Intended outcomes—and therefore, the focus of the study—are best considered within the context of developments in the last 20 years or so, during which two important trends have had an impact on higher education: assessment and, relatedly, accountability.

Traditional assessment activities have provided feedback to students, faculty members, programs, and colleges. Libraries have not been part of the (presumably continuous improvement) process. When a college or university undertakes to assess its own performance (or the synergistic outcomes of its students, faculty, programs, and services), it is called assessment. When others assess the performance of the college or university, it is accountability—regardless of the clothes in which it is dressed.

Accountability advocates, especially state legislatures, tired of pouring a seemingly inexhaustible stream of money into the sinkhole called higher education, are viewing colleges and universities as factories and higher education as a production process. The calls for accountability are made in the face of widespread disagreement about what colleges are supposed to produce and how to measure the outputs and outcomes of the academic experience. Despite the uncertainties of the debate, measures to determine fiscal efficiency and resource productivity have been created and applied to numerous public and private colleges and universities around the world. Examples of such measures include cost per FTE student and percent of time faculty spend teaching.

It is ironic to acknowledge that although learning is the role of higher education, there is no clear model for assessment (so the colleges and universities can improve their processes—that is, learn) and how to demonstrate to others (accountability—that is, learning from others) the value of a college education. In a similar vein, there is no assessment model to demonstrate the value of research and service of faculty and students to the community, yet each educational institution has some component of teaching, research, and service articulated in its mission statement.

Four powerful questions influence assessment outcomes:

- What is the *purpose* of assessment? Why is the campus focusing on assessment? For instance, the assessment might be done to enhance teaching and learning or might be the response to an external demand for accountability. Remember that assessment is a kind of "action research" that is to inform local action.

- What is the *level* of assessment? Who is to be assessed? Will the research focus on implications for individual students, or must results deliver programmatic outcomes at the course, program, department, campus, or college/university level?

- What is the *focus* of assessment? The outcome scope provides rich choices in research design, ranging from knowledge (breadth and depth), to skills (basic, higher-order, and career-related), to attitudes, to behavioral.[2]

- What assessment *resources* are available?

Combining these questions with Ewell's four dimensions results in the three-dimensional figure shown in Figure 1.1.

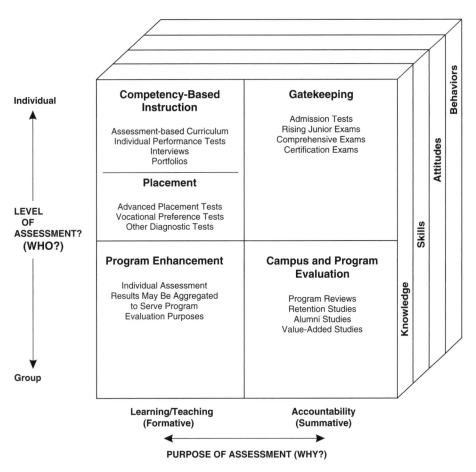

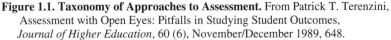

Figure 1.1. Taxonomy of Approaches to Assessment. From Patrick T. Terenzini, Assessment with Open Eyes: Pitfalls in Studying Student Outcomes, *Journal of Higher Education*, 60 (6), November/December 1989, 648.

Cecilia Lopez,[3] the former associate director of the Higher Learning Commission of the North Central Association of Colleges and Schools, has suggested that assessment in the academic environment can become effective if the following characteristics are observed:

- Assessment should be guided by a conceptual framework.

- Assessment activities should be envisioned and implemented according to a plan that is regularly reviewed and updated.

- Assessment activities must have ongoing commitment within the institution rather than occur as episodic events. Collecting, reviewing, analyzing, and utilizing the data from assessing students, programs, departments, and the college and university will result in improvements in student learning and institutional effectiveness.

- Institutions must have the intellectual and fiscal commitment to ensure the ongoing support of an assessment program.

- Integrating the results of assessment activities will result in improvement of student learning and, indirectly, the provision of library and other support services on campus. Communicating and clarifying the intent of the role of assessment for faculty and staff in improving instruction and informing institutional decision making will do much to decease potential anxiety about the process.

A Culture of Assessment

What is a cynic? A man who knows the price of everything and the value of nothing.
—Oscar Wilde[4]

Traditionally, librarians have relied on instincts and experience to make decisions. Alternatively, a library can embrace a "culture of assessment" in which decisions are based on facts, research, and analysis. Others have called a culture of assessment a "culture of evidence" or a "culture of curiosity." The library focuses on planning and delivering services that maximize the anticipated outcomes and impacts for its customers and stakeholders. The library and its staff members have a clear understanding of what customers expect and value. Thus, the collection and analysis of data, even data collected in an ad hoc or unsystematic manner, can be useful in more accurately defining a problem, in revealing activities or processes that may require further study and analysis, as well as in monitoring the progress that is being made to achieve specific goals and objectives.

Even though information in the form of performance measures and statistics should be of great value to any rational decision-making process, much of the information found in a library is[5]

- gathered but has little relevance in the decision-making process;

- gathered for a specific decision, but then not used;

- used to justify a decision (and sometimes gathered after the decision is made);

- requested even though sufficient information is available to make a decision (some data manipulation and analysis may be required);

- not used even though some people will complain about the lack of information; and

- not in itself as important as just having it.

> *Strategic management is not a box of tricks or a bundle of techniques. It is analytical thinking and commitment of resources to action.*
> —Peter Drucker[6]

It would be nice to be able to state that a majority of libraries have developed a "culture of assessment," but sadly that is not the case. And this lack of a culture of assessment is most distressing because the benefits of using assessment as the foundation for decisions will advance the central role of the library on campus. The collection of data can be the catalyst to move a library in the right direction, make improvements in services to improve productivity and lower costs per transaction, improve customer service, and demonstrate the value of the library to its stakeholders.

> *The real question isn't how well you're doing today against your own history, but how well you're doing against your competition.*
> —Donald Kress

In particular, libraries need to shift their inward-looking focus on the collection and its use of input, process, and output measures to measures that evaluate the outcomes or impacts on students and faculty and the larger organizational context. Assuming an outward-looking or customer focus has several implications:

- Customers are the most influential part of an organization, particularly in today's student-centered academic environments.

- Building library "market" on campus requires attracting new customers and retaining existing customers by satisfying—and anticipating—their needs.

- The library organization can't satisfy customer needs unless the library staff understands user needs and preferences.[8]

In addition, a customer focus can encourage library staff to abandon the perspective of the limiting traditional, departmental boundaries and identify holistic, customer-focused solutions.

To achieve the benefits that a "culture of assessment" will bring, Amos Lakos has suggested that

> Libraries must have an organizational environment in which decisions are based on facts, research and analysis, and where services are planned and delivered in ways that maximize the positive outcomes and impacts for customers and stakeholders. A culture of assessment exists in organizations where staff cares to know what results they produce and how those results related to customer expectations. Organization mission, values, structures and systems support behavior that is performance and learning focused.[9]

There are a number of reasons why a culture of assessment is not frequently fostered in any library. Among these are the following:

- *The perception that one can't measure what the library does.* Clearly it is difficult to assess the impact of the library on students and faculty and its larger organizational setting. And since it is difficult, few efforts have been made.

- *Lack of leadership.* The library director and the campus administrators have no understanding of how the use of outcome measures can assist the library in demonstrating the value of the library.

- *The library not having control over its outcomes.* This is true of most academic libraries, but it is still possible to identify outcome measures. One possible outcome measure might be "use of library resources leads to better academic success."

- *The possibility of using such information against the library.* Demonstrating openness and accountability, even when the news is not positive, inspires trust. Being open about what areas need improvement and showing that plans are in place to make enhancements is all that most stakeholders are looking for.

- *Lack of skills.* The librarians and other staff members feel that they do not have the necessary skills to effectively gather statistics and performance measures through the use of surveys, focus groups, observations, and so forth. Such skills can be developed with training.

- *The move to increased demand for electronic resources and services.*

- *Old mental models.* Traditionally, librarians have used input and output measures, which are counts of size and activity, as measures of success. There is scant recognition of the need to determine the impact of the library on the lives of students and faculty through the use of outcome measures.

- *The status quo being preferred.* Some library staff members are not interested in changing or stretching. Their attitude is, "If it ain't broke, don't fix it."

However, it is possible to change libraries so that they move to embrace a culture of assessment in which the following are true:

- The library's mission, planning, and policies are focused on supporting the customer's information and communication needs, and written documents explicitly acknowledge a customer focus.

- Performance measures are included in library planning documents such as strategic plans. Along with identifying a specific set of measures, a time frame for achieving targets for each measure is defined.

- Leadership is key. The library director and the top management team are committed to supporting assessment. Use of assessment tools is supported, and staff at all levels are encouraged to participate. Assessment is a part of the normal work process.

- Continuous communication with customers is maintained through needs assessment, quality outcome, and satisfaction measurements.

- All library programs, services, and products are evaluated for quality and impact. The focus of evaluation includes quality assessments as well as the actual outcomes or impacts of the library on the lives of users. Staff understand that the assessment will focus on the processes, procedures, and services rather than on evaluation of individuals.

- Staff have the opportunity and resources to improve their skills to better serve users.

- Assessment efforts are celebrated and rewarded. Initial activities are those that will be successful in the short term so that people will become supportive and enthusiastic.[10]

> *The choice is clear. Change now and choose our futures. Change later, or not at all, and have no future.*
> —Carla J. Stoffle, Robert Renaud, and Jerilyn R. Veldof. [11]

Important Note

This book is concerned with assessment from the broad perspective. It is not concerned with the evaluation or assessment that an academic library might undertake to understand and improve existing services. The opportunities and perils of undertaking assessment or evaluation activities that focus on internal operations, such as, circulation, interlibrary loan, reference, information literacy instruction, electronic resources, the library's Web page, and technical services, deserve separate treatment. Thus the issues surrounding the evaluation of specific library services are outside the scope of this book.

Organization of the Book

This book provides a compendium of valuable information on research literature and best practices in assessment from an academic institutional point of view as well as an academic library perspective. The intention has been to integrate this wealth of information into a set of tools that can be easily applied in the academic librarian's situation.

Chapter 2—Mission of the College or University

An important first step in the strategic planning process is the preparation of a mission statement. A majority of academic libraries have crafted mission statements. However, despite their length, most of these statements do not address three fundamental questions: Who are we? Where are we going (the vision)? And how will we contribute to the higher education mission of our institution? This chapter identifies the importance and characteristics of a library mission statement within the context of the academic organization's mission statement. With such a guiding statement, library staff can achieve central roles in higher education activities with students and faculty, campus administrators, and other interested stakeholders.

Chapter 3—Model of the Student Educational Process

A model of the student educational process, called the Input-Environment-Output (I-E-O) model, is presented for the purpose of structure. This I-E-O model is used as a structure to summarize a number of research studies that investigated each of the components of the model. Information about the research outcomes can help ensure that library mission statements reflect reality within the higher education model.

Chapter 4—Assessment of Student Learning Outcomes

Academic institutions have used a variety of assessment practices to evaluate their performance. So have libraries. Assessment can take place by focusing on the student, the course, the program or department, and/or the institution. A variety of research methodologies have also been employed, and this literature is summarized in this chapter.

Chapter 5—Assessment of the Library's Contribution to the Educational Process

This chapter reviews research literature pertinent to the library's possible impact on students' educational achievements. Among the topics that are explored are the use of the library, evaluation of library instruction programs, evaluation of information literacy, evaluation of reference services, and "library as place."

Chapter 6—Institutional Assessment of the Research Environment

Assessment of the impact of the research environment within the context of the university is reviewed in this chapter. Among the approaches that have been used are the scholarly peer assessment, an exploration of the individual characteristics of the researcher, and the impact of departmental and institutional characteristics on research.

Chapter 7—Assessment of the Library's Impact on the Research Environment

Although there are a number of ways in which a library could assess its impact on the teaching, learning, and research missions of the higher education environment, several specific methods that have been used to assess the research environment are reviewed and discussed in this chapter.

Chapter 8—Development of a Library Assessment Plan

This chapter presents a step-by-step process to assist the college and research library in developing an assessment plan that both is aligned with and complements the assessment plan of the larger university. Specific suggestions are made as to how the library can begin to determine its contribution to student educational achievement as well as an institution's teaching, learning, and research environment.

Notes

1. Jerry D. Campbell, Changing a Cultural Icon: The Academic Library as a Virtual Destination. *Educause Review*, January/February 2006, 28.

2. Peter T. Ewell. Establishing a Campus-Based Assessment Program, in D. F. Halpre, ed., *Student Outcomes Assessment: What Institutions Stand to Gain*. San Francisco: Jossey-Bass, 1987.

3. Cecilia L. Lopez. Assessment of Student Learning: Challenges and Strategies. *The Journal of Academic Librarianship*, 28 (6), November 2002, 356–67.

4. Oscar Wilde, *Lady Windermere's Fan, Act III*, 1892.

5. W. L. Tetlow. The Pragmatic Imperative of Institutional Research, in J. W. Fimberg and W. F. Lasher, eds. *The Politics and Pragmatics of Institutional Research. New Directions for Institutional Research: No. 38*. San Francisco: Jossey-Bass, 1983, 3–10.

6. Arthur A. Thompson Jr. and A. J. Strickland III. *Crafting and Executing Strategy: Text and Readings*. New York: McGraw-Hill, 2001, 1.

7. Thompson and Strickland. *Crafting and Executing Strategy*, 112.

8. Susan B. Barnard. Implementing Total Quality Management: A Model for Research Libraries. *Journal of Academic Librarianship*, 18, 1993, 57–70.

9. Amos Lakos. Library Management Information Systems in the Client Server Environment: A Proposed New Model, in *Proceedings of the 2nd Northumbria International Conference on Performance Measurement & Libraries & Information Services*. Newcastle, UK: University of Northumbria, 1998, 277–86.

10. Amos Lakos. Culture of Assessment as a Catalyst for Organizational Culture Change in Libraries, in *Proceedings of the Fourth Northumbria International Conference on Performance Measurement in Libraries and Information Service, 12 to 16 August 2001*. Newcastle, UK: University of Northumbria, 2002, 311–20.

11. Carla J. Stoffle, Robert Renaud, and Jerilyn R. Veldof. Choosing Our Futures. *College & Research Libraries*, 57 (3), May 1996, 225.

Mission of the College or University

Stating or articulating the mission of a college or university almost seems axiomatic. Surely it must be obvious what the mission is. After all, a college or university is an educational institution that exists to educate its students. And yet, even a cursory review of mission statements at colleges or universities will reveal some major problems.

The mission statement, sometimes called a purpose statement, is designed to clearly articulate the purposes and values of the organization. The criteria for assessing the effectiveness of the educational process will either be nonexistent or ambiguous unless the organization's goals are clearly defined. A vision statement expresses the library's view of the future and its role in the lives of its customers. A vision statement answers: Where are we going?

The library's mission statement should be able to succinctly answer the following questions: Who are we? Whom do we serve? What roles do we play in the lives of our customers? What are we aiming to accomplish? A good mission statement will include a focus on the customers served by the academic library, indicate the services and/or products provided, and specify how customers benefits.

Some mission statements take a broad view that attempts to answer two fundamental questions: What business are we in? and What business should we be in? However, most organizations separate these two questions into two statements: a mission statement (articulating the present—what we do) and a vision statement (communicating the future—what we *will* do).

> *The typical mission statement is a long, awkward sentence [paragraph, or page] that demonstrates management's inability to think clearly.*
> —Scott Adams[1]

One study found that a clear mission statement was one of four primary characteristics of successful nonprofit organizations.[2] The value of a powerful mission statement is that it can energize library staff members, reduce the need for supervision, and assist in making decisions within the organization. Most often the mission statement is a general declaration of attitude and outlook rather than a specific program of action. Being broad in scope allows alternative objectives and strategies without unduly stifling creativity. An excess of detail could prove to be counterproductive. And more important, criteria of effectiveness are especially ambiguous in organizations that lack clearly defined goals.[3]

The mission of an institution of higher education, at broad and specific levels, serves as the context within which to assess the library's mission. The institution's mission also serves as the foundation for assessment efforts at the institutional, program, and course levels as well as the other support services provided by the institution to its students and faculty. See Figure 2.1 for sample university mission statements.

For example, a comprehensive university in the public sector may have a mission developed in large part by the wider audience needs and interests of the state. Accountability to the state may also include the demonstration of service to the community, success in workforce development, and the ability to attract and keep intellectual resources within the state.

Private colleges may have missions that are focused on providing a liberal arts education or faith-based goals and objectives to a more targeted or focused group. Accountability to the focused group may include the demonstration of community benefit and success in expanding potential or existing group participation. Confusion about the mission of an educational institution may result in misallocated resources and the failure to understand, let alone achieve, desirable goals and objectives.

The complexity of the academic environment that must be confronted when attempting to formulate an appropriate mission statement cannot be overstated. Often competing agendas serve to encourage obfuscation, as illustrated by this list of nine dimensions of organizational effectiveness in an academic environment:

- Student educational satisfaction
- Student academic development
- Student career development
- Student personal development
- Faculty and administrator employment satisfaction
- Professional development and quality of the faculty
- System openness and community interaction
- Ability to acquire resources
- Organizational health[4]

University of Washington Mission Statement

The primary mission of the University of Washington is the preservation, advancement, and dissemination of knowledge. The University preserves knowledge through its libraries and collections, its courses, and the scholarship of its faculty. It advances new knowledge through many forms of research, inquiry and discussion; and disseminates it through the classroom and the laboratory, scholarly exchanges, creative practice, international education, and public service. As one of the nation's outstanding teaching and research institutions, the University is committed to maintaining an environment for objectivity and imaginative inquiry and for the original scholarship and research that ensure the production of new knowledge in the free exchange of facts, theories, and ideas.

To promote their capacity to make humane and informed decisions, the University fosters an environment in which its students can develop mature and independent judgment and an appreciation of the range and diversity of human achievement. The University cultivates in its students both critical thinking and the effective articulation of that thinking.

As an integral part of a large and diverse community, the University seeks broad representation of and encourages sustained participation in that community by its students, its faculty, and its staff. It serves both non-traditional and traditional students. Through its three-campus system and through educational outreach, evening degree, and distance learning, it extends educational opportunities to many who would not otherwise have access to them.

University of Oregon Mission Statement

The University of Oregon is a comprehensive research university that serves its students and the people of Oregon, the nation, and the world through the creation and transfer of knowledge in the liberal arts, the natural and social sciences, and the professions. It is the Association of American Universities flagship institution of the Oregon University System.

The university is a community of scholars dedicated to the highest standards of academic inquiry, learning, and service. Recognizing that knowledge is the fundamental wealth of civilization, the university strives to enrich the public that sustains it through

- a commitment to undergraduate education, with a goal of helping the individual learn to question critically, think logically, communicate clearly, act creatively, and live ethically

- a commitment to graduate education to develop creators and innovators who will generate new knowledge and shape experience for the benefit of humanity

Figure 2.1. Sample University Mission Statements

- a recognition that research, both basic and applied, is essential to the intellectual health of the university, as well as to the enrichment of the lives of Oregonians, by energizing the state's economic, cultural, and political structure
- the establishment of a framework for lifelong learning that leads to productive careers and to the enduring joy of inquiry
- the integration of teaching, research, and service as mutually enriching enterprises that together accomplish the university's mission and support its spirit of community
- the acceptance of the challenge of an evolving social, political, and technological environment by welcoming and guiding change rather than reacting to it
- a dedication to the principles of equality of opportunity and freedom from unfair discrimination for all members of the university community and an acceptance of true diversity as an affirmation of individual identity within a welcoming community
- a commitment to international awareness and understanding, and to the development of a faculty and student body that are capable of participating effectively in a global society
- the conviction that freedom of thought and expression is the bedrock principle on which university activity is based
- the cultivation of an attitude toward citizenship that fosters a caring, supportive atmosphere on campus and the wise exercise of civic responsibilities and individual judgment throughout life
- a continuing commitment to affordable public higher education

The San Diego State University Mission Statement

The mission of San Diego State University shall be to provide well-balanced, high quality education for undergraduate and graduate students and to contribute to knowledge and the solution of problems through excellence and distinction in teaching, research, and service. The university shall impart an appreciation and broad understanding of human experience throughout the world and the ages. This education shall extend to

Diverse cultural legacies,

Accomplishments in many areas, such as the arts and technology,

The advancement of human thought, including philosophy and science,

The development of economic, political, and social institutions, and

The physical and biological evolution of humans and their environment.

Figure 2.1. Sample University Mission Statements (*Continued*)

The university shall accomplish this through its many and diverse departments and interdisciplinary programs in the creative and performing arts, the humanities, the natural and mathematical sciences, and the social and behavioral sciences. Through the President's Shared Vision, students, parents, faculty, staff, administrators, and the community have identified the following five challenges:

1.1 To extend and enhance the university's deep and abiding commitment to academic excellence expressed through superior teaching, research, creative activity, and public service;

1.2 To nurture a learning-centered university that supports the growth and development of the whole person;

1.3 To create a community proud of its diversity and committed to furthering social justice on and off campus;

1.4 To promote the growth, development, and wise use of our human and fiscal resources; and

1.5 To create a global university.

The University of California Berkeley Mission Statement

The University of California Berkeley's fundamental missions are teaching, research and public service.

We teach—educating students at all levels, from undergraduate to the most advanced graduate level. Undergraduate programs are available to all eligible California high-school graduates and community college transfer students who wish to attend the University of California.

Instructional programs at the undergraduate level transmit knowledge and skills to students. At the graduate level, students experience with their instructors the processes of developing and testing new hypotheses and fresh interpretations of knowledge. Education for professional careers, grounded in understanding of relevant sciences, literature and research methods, provides individuals with the tools to continue intellectual development over a lifetime and to contribute to the needs of a changing society.

Through our academic programs, UC helps create an educated workforce that keeps the California economy competitive. And, through University Extension, with a half-million enrollments annually, UC provides continuing education for Californians to improve their job skills and enhance the quality of their lives.

Figure 2.1. Sample University Mission Statements (*Continued*)

We do research—by some of the world's best researchers and brightest students in hundreds of disciplines at its campuses, national laboratories, medical centers and other research facilities around the state. UC provides a unique environment in which leading scholars and promising students strive together to expand fundamental knowledge of human nature, society, and the natural world. Its basic research programs yield a multitude of benefits for California: billions of tax dollars, economic growth through the creation of new products, technologies, jobs, companies and even new industries, agricultural productivity, advances in health care, improvements in the quality of life. UC's research has been vital in the establishment of the Internet and the semiconductor, software and biotechnology industries in California, making substantial economic and social contributions.

We provide public service, which dates back to UC's origins as a land grant institution in the 1860s. Today, through its public service programs and industry partnerships, UC disseminates research results and translates scientific discoveries into practical knowledge and technological innovations that benefit California and the nation.

UC's agricultural extension programs serve hundreds of thousands of Californians in every county in the state.

Open to all Californians, UC's libraries, museums, performing arts spaces, gardens and science centers are valuable public resources and community gathering places.

California State University San Marcos Mission Statement

The University's active involvement in public-school partnerships and professional development institutes help strengthen the expertise of teachers and the academic achievement of students in communities throughout California.

California State University San Marcos focuses on the student as an active participant in the learning process. Students work closely with a faculty of active scholars and artists whose commitment to sustained excellence in teaching, research, and community partnership enhances student learning. The university offers rigorous undergraduate and graduate programs distinguished by exemplary teaching, innovative curricula, and the application of new technologies. CSUSM provides a range of services that responds to the needs of a student body with diverse backgrounds, expanding student access to an excellent and affordable education. As a public university, CSUSM grounds its mission in the public trust, alignment with regional needs, and sustained enrichment of the intellectual, civic, economic, and cultural life of our region and state.

Figure 2.1. Sample University Mission Statements (*Continued*)

Kim Cameron found that effectiveness in one domain may not necessarily translate into effectiveness in another domain. For example, high effectiveness among faculty members (as evidenced by a large number of published articles, books, and research reports) may result in poor teaching quality, little time for students, and use of graduate assistants rather than professors in the classroom.

Addressing the issue of organizational effectiveness when faced with declining fiscal resources, Kim Cameron and John Smart found that academic institutions with declining resources are as effective as institutions with abundant resources.[5] However, colleges and universities that develop dysfunctional attributes, such as centralized decision making, neglecting planning, strong resistance to change, high administrative turnover, and not setting priorities when cutbacks are made, perform less effectively.

Reviewing a number of academic library mission statements reveals that the most frequently cited purposes were "to serve the needs of users" or "to provide access to information." Most statements identify the means the library uses to provide services, that is, by "providing the collections," "organizing the resources," "providing public services," and "providing instruction in the use of the library or information literacy." A small sample of academic library mission statements is shown in Figure 2.2. With the exception of the University of Washington and the University of Oregon, these sample mission statements are simply too long and confusing. It is difficult to determine what the focus of the library is and how the library's mission is aligned with the university's.

One overriding problem with a majority of library mission statements is that they become "motherhood" and "apple pie" statements—generalized statements of goodness with which no one could possibly disagree and that no one could measure. Such an approach has little meaning except perhaps to persuade librarians of their value to themselves or to convince university administrators of the value of libraries. Renowned teacher and author Peter Drucker has observed that some organizations make the mistake of turning their mission statement into "hero sandwiches of good intentions."[6]

Clarifying and communicating the mission assures the library's various stakeholders about why the library is doing what it does and provides a rationale and structure to the library's future decisions and actions. It is not the intention of this work to recommend ways to develop a library mission statement here, as this is normally done in a broader context of developing or updating a strategic plan.[7]

The University of Washington Libraries enriches the quality of life and advances intellectual discovery by connecting people with knowledge.

The University of Oregon Libraries enriches the student learning experience, encourages exploration and research at all levels, and contributes to advancements in access to scholarly resources.

The University of California, San Diego Libraries select, acquire, manage, deliver, and preserve a diversified and broad range of information resources for UCSD students, faculty, and staff in support of the instructional, research, patient care, and public service goals of the University. The Libraries deliver programs that support teaching and learning, foster information competence, and provide expertise, tools, and services to facilitate access to and management of the campus' scholarly information assets. The Libraries' welcoming facilities provide an environment conducive to study and learning, and foster a sense of intellectual discovery and community on the UCSD campus.

The Library at San Diego State University is the main intellectual resource supporting the teaching, research, and service functions of the University. It strives to meet the needs of an ever-changing world of information, technology, and users. To accomplish its mission, the Library aspires to the highest quality in service, instruction, collection, staff, and environment.

The Library supports the teaching function of the University by providing the information resources and services needed by undergraduate and graduate students in pursuit of their education. It cooperates with faculty in their goals of providing a high quality educational experience. The Library's collection is shaped by the range and level of courses offered, and is augmented by appropriate information delivery services.

The Library recognizes that its patrons are becoming more diverse in their backgrounds, interests, and methods of research. Diversity of patrons comes in many forms cultural, ethnic, age, gender, socioeconomic, and those with disabilities. To accommodate the needs of all patrons, this diversity must be reflected in the Library's services and the development of its information resources.

The UC Berkeley Library connects students and scholars to the world of information and ideas. With a daily commitment to excellence and innovation, we select and create, organize and protect, provide and teach access to resources that are relevant to our campus programs and pursuits.

The Library is committed to providing a learning environment which supports the information needs of the Cal State University, San Marcos community. Our services, collections, teaching and community outreach honor and reflect diverse perspectives, learning styles and ways of knowing. With the help of innovative technologies, our staff aggressively select, acquire, provide access and deliver resources and instruction that support the lifelong learning needs of our students and community. The Library upholds and practices the principles of the CSUSM Mission Statement and the Library Bill of Rights, endorsed by the American Library Association.

Figure 2.2. Sample Library Mission Statements

However, most academic library mission statements are simply too long, don't reflect the actual mission of the library, and articulate the processes the library uses to deliver services. The goal should be a succinct statement about what the library does—it's best if the statement can be printed on a T-shirt! The statement should be clear, memorable, and short. This is no small undertaking.

Yet the mission statements of most academic libraries fail to focus on the impacts and benefits for their customers. A notable exception is that of the Indiana University Purdue University at Indianapolis (IUPUI) Library, which is derived from and aligned with the university's mission statement:

- To promote excellence in learning

- To serve as a gateway to information vital for research and scholarship

- To create unique scholarly resources with an emphasis on philanthropic studies, IUPUI generated research, and materials relating to central Indiana

- To enhance the availability of scholarly information for the residents of central Indiana.

Academic libraries must be able to express how the library is unique and how it adds value and contributes to the intellectual life of the university. Unfortunately, most libraries operate on a premise that the services they provide are needed and important. The books are ordered, databases are subscribed to, staff show up to perform their jobs, and buildings are remodeled or built. But is the library really carrying out its purpose? Is the library adding value to the intellectual lives of its students, faculty, and staff?

The mission statement offers the opportunity to identify the distinctive purposes of the library. This framework establishes the context for the evaluation of library services and informs in terms of user satisfaction. If so aligned, outcomes could permit the organization to navigate nimbly amid a constantly changing environment.

There is danger in ignoring the mission statement, since it is used by those who evaluate the library and make ongoing decisions about budgets.[8] On the other hand, a relevant and compelling mission statement clearly articulates how the library meets the needs of its parent institution through advancing the institutional mission.

One recent study examined the presence of a mission statement at all of the Association of Research Libraries (ARL) member Web sites. Despite the fact that 78 percent of the libraries have a mission statement on their Web sites, the vast majority of these libraries do not place their mission among the more visible parts of the Web site (often a search is required to retrieve the library's mission statement).[9] Making the mission statement more visible, assuming it is good, would help remind everyone of the principal focus of the library. As Stephen Covey has observed: "The main thing is to keep the main thing the main thing."[10]

Accreditation

Accreditation is perhaps the best known seal of collegiate quality. The purposes of accreditation are to foster self-improvement and quality assurance and are the cornerstone of self-regulation. Rather than an emphasis on meeting minimum standards of quality, regional accreditation organizations focus on institutional capacity and the will, culture, and ability to improve continuously.

Judgments of institutional quality and effectiveness are determined in relationship to the institution's mission and goals, the adequacy and effectiveness of its resources, and the manner and degree to which a university uses assessment to determine the degree to which its goals and mission are being achieved. The accreditation process begins from the foundation of the institution's own mission and goals.

Formerly, the accreditation evaluation process proceeded on the assumption that the quality of implied institutional outcomes was dependent on the quality and quantity of institutional "inputs." More recently, external constituencies have become skeptical of the validity of judgments of quality based on a review of institutional resources and intentions and have demanded evidence of institutional outcomes and actual results. There has been a shift of values from a social model that a collegiate education benefits individuals directly and society indirectly to an economic model that requires a real return on investments.[11] Some institutions are being asked to demonstrate the value of the college or university and its contribution to the "public good."

The implications of this shift of values cannot be overemphasized. The calls for increased accountability and the documenting of results in terms that are understandable to stakeholders and funding decision makers has many institutions of higher education scrambling to formulate an assessment plan. Not only does the pressure exist for the university as a whole to demonstrate results, but other units on campus, including the library, are being asked for an assessment plan that goes beyond what most libraries have relied on in the past.

In accord with its mission, each institution of higher education is expected to formulate a plan that provides a comprehensive assessment of outcomes and uses the results of assessment to improve planning and come closer to achieving its stated mission.

The implication for academic libraries is that the accreditation organizations are less concerned about measuring traditional library inputs and are moving to asking for measures that focus on the impact of the library in the lives of students, faculty, researchers, and others. This shift toward determining outputs is evidenced by the use of such phrases as "evaluation of student performance," and "evidence of student learning," found in some of the regional accreditation standards.

Assessing student needs, perceptions, and levels of satisfaction and demonstrating that the findings are used for service improvement is clearly a fundamental expectation of the regional accreditation commissions.[12] This will require that a library create an assessment plan that will capture and use this information to better shape library services.

Notes

1. Cited in M. B. Line. What Do People Need of Libraries, and How Can We Find Out? *Australian Academic & Research Libraries,* 27, June 1996, 79.

2. E. B. Knauft, Reneeee Burger, and Sandra Gray. *Profiles of Excellence.* San Francisco: Jossey-Bass, 1991.

3. Kim S. Cameron. A Study of Organizational Effectiveness and Its Predictors. *Management Science,* 32 (1), 1986, 87–112.

4. Kim Cameron. Measuring Organizational Effectiveness in Institutions of Higher Education. *Administrative Science Quarterly,* 23, December 1978, 604–29.

5. Kim Cameron and John Smart. Maintaining Effectiveness Amid Downsizing and Decline in Institutions of Higher Education. *Research in Higher Education,* 39 (1), 1998, 65–86.

6. Peter Drucker. *Managing the Non-Profit Organization.* New York: HarperBusiness, 1990, 5.

7. For information on strategic planning, see Joseph R. Matthews. *Strategic Planning and Management for Library Managers.* Westport, CT: Libraries Unlimited, 2005.

8. Gary Hartzell. Promises You Can't Keep. *School Library Journal,* 9, 1988, 30–36.

9. Triveni Kuchi. Communicating Mission: An Analysis of Academic Library Web Sites. *The Journal of Academic Librarianship,* 32 (2), March 2006, 148–54.

10. Stephen Covey. *First Things First.* New York: Simon & Schuster, 1994.

11. Peter T. Ewell. A Matter of Integrity: Accountability and the Future of Self-Regulation. *Change,* 26 (6), 1994, 16–23.

12. Bonnie Gratch-Lindauer. Comparing the Regional Accreditation Standards: Outcomes Assessment and Other Trends. *The Journal of Academic Librarianship,* 28 (1), January–March 2002, 14–25.

Chapter

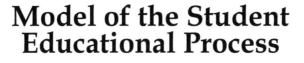

Model of the Student
Educational Process

College students are in a continuous state of growth and change. Others, not choosing a career path that includes college, are also growing and changing as they experience life. As students advance toward their goal of a college degree, researchers are confronted with an important task of determining what difference college attendance makes in the life of an individual. Merely assessing the degree of growth and change between the time an individual enters college and graduation, and equating that growth to the impact of college, life fails to understand the complexity of assessing the impact of the college experience.

While some change and growth is clearly the result of the collegiate experience, other factors are also involved. For example, the individual naturally is maturing and has other experiences outside the college environment that affect maturation.

Conceptually it helps if we can use a model that will assist us in understanding the issues surrounding the collegiate assessment process. There is no lack of theories or models of student change in college. Among these are

- psychosocial theories, which view individual development as a process that involves the accomplishments as a series of "tasks";[1]
- cognitive-structural models, which seek to describe the process of change;[2]
- typological models, which emphasize the distinctive but stable differences among individuals and may focus on cognitive style, learning style, maturity level, personality, or sociodemographic characteristics;[3] and
- college impact models of student change, which focus on the process and origins of change. Among the more well-known models are
  - Alexander Astin's Theory of "Involvement," which suggests that students learn by becoming involved,[4]
  - Vincent Tinto's Theory of Student Departure, which seeks to explain the college student attrition process,[5] and
  - Earnest Pascarella's General Model for Assessing Change, shown in Figure 3.1, which suggests that student growth is a function of the direct and indirect effects of five major sets of variables.[6]

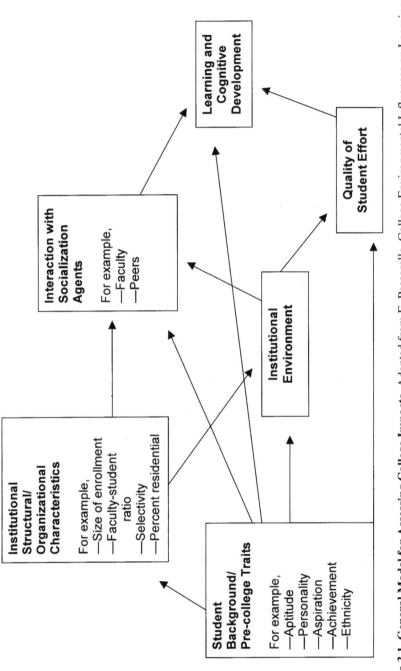

Figure 3.1. General Model for Assessing College Impacts. Adapted from E. Pascarella, College Environmental Influences on Learning and Cognitive Development: A Critical Review and Synthesis, in J. Smart, ed., *Higher Education: Handbook of Theory and Research, Volume 1*. New York: Agathon, 1985.

Another model, developed by Astin and used for a relatively long period of time by a number of academic assessment researchers, is called the Input-Environment-Output (I-E-O) model. This model is similar to the input-process-output-outcome model often found in library literature. The components of this I-E-O model, shown in Figure 3.2, include:

- *Inputs,* which refer to the student characteristics at the time of starting college

- *Environment,* which refers to the various programs, services, faculty, peers, policies, and other educational experiences encountered by the student. Note that only a few of the situational factors are shown in the figure.

- *Outcomes,* which refer to the student characteristics after exposure to the collegiate environment.

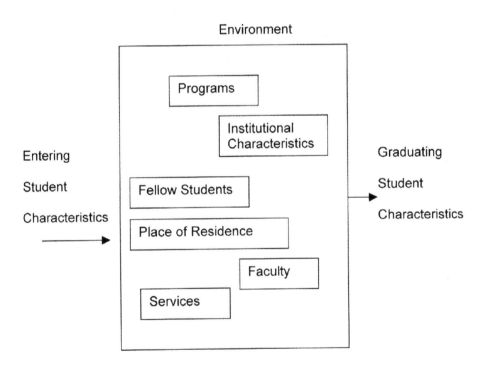

Figure 3.2. The Input-Environment-Output Model

A variation of the I-E-O model, shown in Figure 3.3, adds a feedback loop so that improvements can be made in the education experience (presumably the improvements will either make better graduates or mean a greater number of students will graduate, or both).

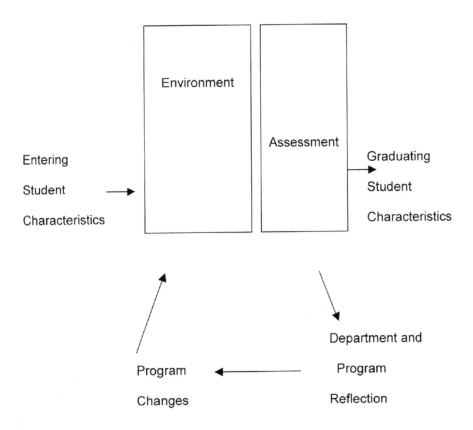

Figure 3.3. The Input-Environment-Output Model with Feedback

Each of the components of the I-E-O model is reviewed in the following sections.

Inputs

Among the many variables included in the "inputs" portion of the I-E-O model are intelligence of the student, subjects studied in high school, educational success in high school, planned career choice, student demographic characteristics, parental education and income, and student socialization skills.[7] During the 1990s aptitude test scores rose, and a record number of high school students are now taking advanced placement exams.[8]

Environmental Variables

American higher education institutions are typically classified along two dimensions: type (highest degree offered, e.g., four-year college, university) and control (source of governance, e.g., public, Protestant, Roman Catholic, nonsectarian). Other measures and characteristics that could be included in the analysis are size of the institution, student-faculty ratio, percent of graduate students in the total student body, average faculty salary, taxonomy of curricular programs, historically black colleges, colleges for women, diversity of the student body, campus support services, percent of students who live on-campus, availability of financial aid, the amount of time faculty and students interact with one another, and research orientation of the campus.

Outcomes

Attempting to identify the overall impact of college attendance and graduation is challenging. College impact is a broad concept that encompasses all the varieties of college experiences and attempts to compare their effects with the result of not attending college. Some researchers have looked at the differences between those who attend college and those who do not. Others have looked at the sources of systematic influence on student development: degree of exposure to college (time and intensity of exposure), maturation, and social change.

Analysis of the I-E-O Model

Reporting the results of a large national longitudinal study, Alexander Astin presented his analysis of the data collected by the Cooperative Institutional Research Program in *What Matters in College?* Data for this longitudinal study were gathered in 1985 and again in 1989/1990. Cooperative Institutional Research Program (CIRP) is a national longitudinal study of the American higher education system. The CIRP is the nation's largest and oldest empirical study of higher education, involving data on some 1,800 institutions and over 11 million students. It is regarded as the most comprehensive source of information on college students.

The peer group has a pervasive effect on the individual college student's development. Every aspect of the student's development—cognitive and affective, psychological and behavioral—is affected by the peer group. Students change their values, behavior, and academic plans in the direction of the central orientation of their peer group. And the peer group's values, attitudes, self-concept, and socioeconomic status are much more important determinants of how a student will develop than are the abilities, religious orientation, or racial composition of the peer group.

Not surprisingly, hours spent studying are positively related to almost all academic outcomes—retention, graduating with honors, standardized test scores, enrolling in graduate school, and so forth. Students involved with cooperative learning are more successful than their counterparts since they are held accountable by their peers for achieving a minimum of learning outcomes and assist their peers in mastering the course content.[9]

Two faculty characteristics—research orientation and student orientation—have substantial effects on student development. Attending a college with a heavy research orientation—in which the faculty is rewarded for scholarship, not teaching prowess—increases student dissatisfaction and has a negative impact on measures of cognitive and affective development. Conversely, attending a college that is strongly oriented toward student development shows the opposite effects.

Once peer group and faculty characteristics are taken into account, institutional type and control have little effect on student development outcomes. Arthur Chickering and Zelda Gamson suggest that the quantity and quality of student-faculty interaction, use of active learning techniques, providing prompt feedback, having high expectations of student achievement, and encouraging a respect for diverse talents and ways of learning leads to high levels of student engagement and academic success.[10] A student's academic achievements are not influenced by the intellectual level of his or her peers, by the level of academic competitiveness, or by the financial resources of the institution.[11]

A true core curriculum (one that requires students to take exactly the same general education courses) results in high satisfaction levels on student development and positive effects on leadership, according to Chickering and Gamson. Yet the vast majority of colleges and universities rely on a cafeteria-style approach to fulfilling general education requirements (take three classes from Category A, take four from Category B, and so forth).

Learning, academic performance, and retention are positively associated with academic involvement, involvement with faculty, and participation with student peer groups. And not surprisingly, overall academic performance is directly related to the amount of time that students devote to studying.[12] Growth in a particular area of knowledge or skill is proportional to the number of courses taken that focus on a particular skill or knowledge. Typically freshman-to-senior gains for general verbal skills are about 21 percentile points, general mathematical skills are 10 percentile points, and specific subject matter knowledge increases some 30 percentile points.[13]

A significant proportion of college students drop out during or following their first year. The overall dropout rate for all colleges consistently falls at 26 to 27 percent, based on ACT surveys (private colleges have slightly lower rates, while pubic colleges and universities have slightly higher rates).[14] The implication of these dropout rates are that only six out of every ten entering full-time freshmen will graduate from college within six years. The top three retention practices that have the greatest impact on student retention are a freshmen university orientation course for credit, a tutoring program, and advising interventions with selected student populations.[15]

A recent study examined the relationships between student engagement as measured by the National Survey of Student Engagement (NSSE) and selected measures of success in colleges for students from different racial and ethnic backgrounds. This "Connecting the Dots" study found that

- engagement has positive, modest effects on grades and persistence for students from different racial and ethnic backgrounds, even after controlling for key precollege variables;

- engagement has compensatory effects on first-year grades and persistence to the second year of college at the same college or university for historically underserved students; and

- the NSSE survey works equally well for students of color and white students in different institutional contexts, such as predominantly white institutions, historically black colleges and universities, and Hispanic-serving institutions.[16]

Generally, students become more positive about their academic and social competencies and develop a greater sense of self-worth and value as they progress through their undergraduate careers.[17] There are general increases in students' freedom from the influences of others, in non-authoritarian thinking and tolerance for other people and their views, in intellectual orientation to problem solving, and in maturity in interpersonal relations.[18]

Involvement in extracurricular activities and the extent and quality of interaction with student peers and faculty have a positive influence on persistence, educational aspirations, bachelor's degree attainment, and graduate school attendance.[19] Forms of involvement that isolate the student from peers or physically remove the student from the campus—living at home, commuting, being employed off campus, being a full-time employee, and watching television—negatively affect student development.

A summary of what affects various student outcomes is shown in Table 3.1. Compared to entering freshmen, college graduates have better oral and written communication skills, are better critical thinkers, will use reason and evidence to address ill-structured problems, and can develop sophisticated abstract frameworks to deal with complexity.[20]

Table 3.1 Summary of Effects on Student Outcomes*

Student Outcomes	Positively Affected by
Academic performance	Student orientation of faculty
	Merit-based scholarship
Social activism	Activism and community orientation
	Peer socioeconomic status
Feeling overwhelmed	Engineering major
	Outside work of peers
Liberalism	Degree of peer and faculty liberalism
Developing a meaningful philosophy of life	Social activism and community orientation
Contributing to scientific theory	Science and health profession majors
	Required internships
Being very well off financially	Materialism and status orientation of peers
Joining social fraternity or sorority	Leaving home to attend college
	Materialism and status orientation of peers
	Percentage of peers with merit-based scholarships
Critical thinking ability	Humanities orientation
	Peer socioeconomic status
	Faculty-student orientation
Analytical and problem-solving skills	Science and engineering majors
	Faculty-student orientation
	Positive attitude by faculty toward general education program
Writing skills	Humanities orientation
	Psychology, social science, and arts and humanities majors
	Faculty-student orientation
	"Progressive" general education curriculum
Preparation for graduate or professional school	Faculty-student orientation
	Peer socioeconomic status

*Adapted from Alexander W. Astin, *What Matters in College? Four Critical Years Revisited.* San Francisco: Jossey-Bass, 1993.

Educational attainment is an important determinant of job status, career mobility, and advancement and is largely independent of gender. A bachelor's degree confers an advantage in occupational status over and above graduating from high school.[21] As a consequence, a bachelor's degree provides somewhere between a 20 and 40 percent earnings advantage when compared to a high school diploma. In addition, the student's major field of study has a significant impact on early career earnings.[22]

Yet the academic community is in much turmoil and coming under increasing pressure from the funding decision makers. Increasingly the perception is that a college degree is much diminished in value, as a recent report states:

> Many students graduate having accumulated whatever number of courses is required, but still lacking a coherent body of knowledge or any inkling as to how one sort of information might relate to others. And all too often they graduate without knowing how to think logically, write clearly, or speak coherently. The university has given too little that will be of real value beyond a credential that will help them find their first jobs. And with larger and larger numbers of their peers holding the same paper in their hands, even that credential has lost much of its potency.[23]

In September 2006 a draft of the Spelling Commission report noted that the world is catching up to the standards of the United States and, in some cases, surpassing U.S. academic excellence. And this is happening at a time when education is more important than ever to the collective prosperity of the United States. The commission recommended that

> Accreditation agencies should make performance outcomes, including completion rates and student learning, the core of their assessment as a priority over inputs or processes. A framework that aligns and expands existing accreditation standards should be established to (i) allow comparisons among institutions regarding learning outcomes and other performance measures, (ii) encourage innovation and continuous improvement, and (iii) require institutions and programs to move toward world-class quality relative to specific missions and report measurable progress in relationship to their national and international peers. In addition, this framework should require that the accreditation process be more open and accessible by making the findings of final reviews easily accessible to the public and increasing the proportion of public and private sector representatives in the governance of accrediting organizations and as members of review teams. Accreditation, once primarily a private relationship between an agency and an institution, now has such important

> public policy implications that accreditor's must continue and speed up their efforts towards transparency where this affects public ends.[24]

The vast majority of studies that examine the impact of college life on student development do not examine the impact of the library in the lives of students or faculty. The study reported by Astin is no exception.

A great deal of the educational assessment literature has been reviewed and synthesized. One synthesis identified the best practices associated with improving the educational experience of students. Chickering and Gamson identified seven principles that colleges and universities should be adopting in order to improve the quality of a student's educational experience:[25]

1. *Encouraging Contacts between Students and Faculty.* The amount of and quality of student-faculty contact helps students get through rough times and keeps them motivated.

2. *Developing Reciprocity and Cooperation among Students.* Learning is enhanced when it is a team effort, as in a relay, rather than a solo event. Working with others increases involvement, improves thinking, and deepens understanding.

3. *Using Active Learning Techniques.* Students comprehend more and can apply the knowledge they learn when they have an opportunity to reflect on what is being learned rather than memorizing material and regurgitating it to complete a test.

4. *Giving Prompt Feedback.* Receiving quality feedback helps keep the student focused on learning.

5. *Emphasizing Time on Task.* Allocating realistic amounts of time means effective learning for students.

6. *Communicating High Expectations.* Expecting students to do well becomes a self-fulfilling prophecy.

7. *Respecting Diverse Talents and Ways of Learning.* Students bring a variety of talents and learning styles to college. They need opportunities to showcase their talents in ways that work for them.

An academic library might partner with faculty and other departments on campus to explore ways that the library could contribute to these best practices.

Notes

1. See, for example, E. Erickson. *Identity: Youth and Crisis*. New York: Norton, 1968; and Arthur Chickering. *Education and Identity*. San Francisco: Jossey-Bass, 1969.

2. See Jean Piaget. Intellectual Evolution from Adolescence to Adulthood. *Human Development*, 15, 1972, 1–12; William Perry. Cognitive and Ethical Growth, in A. Chickering & Associates, eds., *The Modern American College: Responding to the New Realities of Diverse Students and a Changing Society*. San Francisco: Jossey-Bass, 1981; and Lawrence Kohlberg. *The Meaning and Measurement of Moral Development*. Worcester, MA: Clark University Press, 1981.

3. See, for example, R. Rogers. Student Development in Administration and Leadership, in U. Delworth and G. Hanson, eds. *Student Affairs: Actualizing Student Development in Higher Education*. San Francisco: Jossey-Bass, 1989; and Isabel Myers and M. McCaulley. *Manual: A Guide to the Development and Use of Myers-Briggs Type Indicator*. Palo Alto, CA: Consulting Psychologists Press, 1985.

4. Alexander Astin. *Achieving Educational Excellence: A Critical Assessment of Priorities and Practices in Higher Education*. San Francisco: Jossey-Bass, 1985.

5. V. Tinto. *Leaving College: Rethinking the Causes and Cures of Student Attrition*. Chicago: University of Chicago Press, 1987.

6. E. Pascarella. College Environmental Influences on Learning and Cognitive Development: A Critical Review and Synthesis, in J. Smart, ed., *Higher Education: Handbook of Theory and Research, Volume 1*. New York: Agathon, 1985.

7. Unless otherwise noted, the data presented in this chapter come from Alexander W. Astin. *What Matters in College? Four Critical Years Revisited*. San Francisco: Jossey-Bass, 1993. Astin used descriptive data from the Cooperative Institutional Research Program about 309 institutions (4,093 students) and longitudinal environmental outcomes data about 217 institutions and 24,847 students.

8. Neil Howe and William Strauss. *Millennials Rising: The Next Generation*. New York: Vintage Books, 2000.

9. Alexander W. Astin. What Matters in College? *Liberal Education*, 79 (4), Fall 1993, 4–16.

10. Arthur Chickering and Zelda Gamson. Seven Principles for Good Practice in Undergraduate Education. *AAHE Bulletin*, 39 (7), 1987, 3–7.

11. Alexander W. Astin. Undergraduate Achievement and Institutional "Excellence." *Science*, 161, August 16, 1968, 661–68.

12. *National Survey of Student Engagement. 2000 through 2005.* Bloomington, IN: National Survey of Student Engagement. Available at http://nsse.iub.edu/redirect.cfm?target= (accessed March 21, 2007).

13. Ernest T. Pascarella and Patrick T. Terenzini. *How College Affects Students: Findings and Insights from Twenty Years of Research.* San Francisco: Jossey-Bass, 1991, 107–11.

14. Data available at http://www.act.org/path/policy/pdf/retain_charts.pdf (accessed March 21, 2007).

15. Wesley R. Habley and Randy McClanahan. *What Works in Student Retention.* Washington, DC: ACT, 2004.

16. George D. Kuh, Jillian Kinzie, Ty Cruce, Rick Shoup, and Robert M. Gonyea. *Connecting the Dots: Multi-Faceted Analyses of the Relationships between Student Engagement Results from the NSSE, and the Institutional Practices and Conditions that Foster Student Success.* Bloomington: Indiana University Bloomington, Center for Postsecondary Research, January 2007. Available at http://nsse.iub.edu/pdf/Connecting_the_Dots_Report.pdf (accessed March 21, 2007).

17. Pascarella and Terenzini, *How College Affects Students,* 201–9.

18. Pascarella and Terenzini, *How College Affects Students,* 257–64.

19. Pascarella and Terenzini, *How College Affects Students,* 416–21.

20. Pascarella and Terenzini, *How College Affects Students,* 155–60.

21. Pascarella and Terenzini, *How College Affects Students,* 487–95.

22. Pascarella and Terenzini, *How College Affects Students,* 529–33.

23. Boyer Commission on Educating Undergraduates in the Research University. *Reinventing Undergraduate Education: A Blueprint for America's Research Universities.* Stony Brook: State University of New York at Stony Book, 1998,

24. *The Spelling Commission Report.* Washington, DC: Department of Education, September 2006. Available at http://www.de.gov (accessed March 21, 2007).

25. Arthur Chickering and Zelda Gamson. *Seven Principles for Good Practice in Higher Education.* San Francisco: Jossey-Bass, 1987. See also Arthur Chickering and Zelda Gamson. *Applying the Seven Principles for Good Practice in Undergraduate Education.* San Francisco: Jossey-Bass, 1991.

Chapter

4

Assessment of Student Learning Outcomes

The purpose of this chapter is to review the literature of how academic institutions have historically used assessment to determine the impact of education on the life of a student. Assessment efforts can be made at several levels and use a variety of methodologies, which are reviewed here. With this as background, chapter 5 discusses the library's role in the educational process.

The assessment of students, whether done informally or using more structured techniques, has been around for centuries—perhaps as far back as Plato and Aristotle. Yet the challenge to clearly identify student outcomes has been vexing professors, instructors, and administrators for a long time.

With few exceptions, the primary stimulus for assessment activities in a college revolves around the periodic visits of an accreditation team or responding to issues raised by the institution's governing board or the legislature. The real, or perceived, threat of losing accreditation forces an institution to pay some attention to the issue of assessment. There are seven regional accrediting organizations.[1]

The Higher Learning Commission (HLC) is part of the North Central Association of Colleges and Schools and is one of seven regional institutional accrediting agencies in the United States. Through its commissions it accredits, and thereby grants membership to, educational institutions in the North Central region of the United States. The Higher Learning Commission recently adopted new criteria for accreditation along with three cross-cutting issues of diversity, assessment, and general education, which must be addressed as part of the accreditation process. The accreditation criteria include the following:

1. *Mission and Integrity*—The organization works to fulfill its mission through processes and structures that involve the board, administration, faculty, staff, and students.

2. *Preparing for the Future*—The organization allocates resources and has evaluation and assessment processes to demonstrate its ability to improve the quality of education and respond to future challenges and opportunities.

3. *Student Learning and Effective Teaching*—An institution clearly states its goals for student learning outcomes for each educational program.

4. *Acquiring, Creating, and Applying Knowledge*—An institution promotes a life of learning for its students, faculty, and staff by fostering and supporting inquiry, creativity, and practice that are consistent with its mission.

5. *Engagement and Service*—The organization identifies its constituencies and serves them in valuable ways.

Student success starts with an institutional mission that espouses the importance of talent development and then enacts this vision.
—George Kuh et al.[2]

Assessment provides the opportunity for faculty and administrators to discover the fit between institutional or programmatic expectations for student achievement and patterns of actual student achievement. Assessment becomes a lens that allows an institution to focus light on how well it is doing, as evidenced by its students' work, and then make strategic responses or adjustments to improve the educational service delivery. Assessment should never be viewed as an end in itself but rather as a vehicle for educational improvement.

Student assessment can be done at a number of different levels, including

- Individual student,
- Course,
- Department or program, and
- College or university.

Each of these levels is discussed in greater detail in the following sections.

The Individual Student Level

The focus on individual student assessment is to ensure that the student has mastered the content of a course or is making satisfactory progress toward earning a degree. Typically, an instructor will use a variety of methods to assess the degree to which the student has understood and retained the content of the course. The instructor may use tests (in their many standardized or locally developed forms) or require a student to make an oral or multimedia presentation, complete a project, submit one or more written papers, prepare an analysis of a case study, develop a portfolio of work, and so forth. The result of the assessment is the grade earned by the student. Yet for many students, perhaps a majority, the only feedback they receive is a single score on the final examination (and perhaps a score for a mid-term examination).

Tests of basic skills such as reading, writing, speaking, and listening are often used for course advisement and placement purposes when the student first enters an institution. These tests can form the foundation or baseline for assessment purposes to determine the impact of the university on the lives of its graduates. Some of these standardized tests are discussed in a later section of this chapter.

A number of experts suggest that it is important to have more than a single measure when preparing an assessment. Building assessment into a course as an ongoing, iterative process in a course requires considerable effort on the part of the instructor, but the effort will bear real fruit as the students and instructor work collaboratively to achieve some common goals.

National standardized tests should not be used unless they provide relevant information about individual student achievement in the major, particularly if the material covered in the major is not covered by the standardized test. While national standardized tests do provide comparative information, they may not relate to the goals and objectives established by the college or department. In some cases, colleges and universities have integrated assessment into the fabric and culture of the institution, and locally developed exams are scored "objectively" by many of the faculty.

Course Level

Developing statements of intended learning outcomes for each course is an important foundational step in the assessment process. Many teachers and instructors, perhaps a majority, have not developed statements of outcomes. Ideally, student learning outcomes should be student-focused rather than professor-focused. Such statements should articulate what students should know, understand, believe, and be able to do as a result of their course experience.[3] Ideally the learning outcomes focus on the learning resulting from the activity rather than on the activity itself.

Course level assessment is often called *formative evaluation*. The purpose of formative evaluation is to validate or ensure that the goals of the instruction are being achieved and to improve the instruction, if necessary, by means of identification and subsequent remediation of problematic aspects.

One evaluation technique used to assess a course and the methods used to impart the course content is to have a panel review and rate the quality of the papers submitted by students. The assessment of the papers takes into account such criteria as the quality of the writing, the logic used to make and defend a position, the quality of research as evidenced by the choice of citations, the range of journals and scholars used for citations, and so forth. This active learning approach engages students in learning.

Another technique involves a peer review process. Typically the instructor completes a self-examination using a standard that documents best practices. After this, the department head or an appointed department faculty member will review the course. The college or university may also use a peer review team composed of faculty members from other departments.

Department Level

Assessment activities at the departmental level are intended to determine the degree to which students are mastering the materials presented in the required and optional courses. Some assessment experts have suggested that ideally student learning outcomes should be aligned at the course, academic program, and institutional levels. The cumulative effect that students experience as they move through lessons, units, and courses should reinforce the intended student learning outcomes.

A department level perspective typically uses a *summative evaluation* method. A summative evaluation looks at more than one learner's performance to see how well a group did on a learning task that utilized specific learning materials and methods. A summative evaluation might compare the same course taught by different instructors, using different teaching methods, or taught to various groups of students.

> *When the cook tastes the soup, that's formative; when the guests taste the soup, that's summative.*
>
> —Robert Stakes[4]

An assessment technique employed by a number of college departments is the departmental comprehensive exam.[5] Some have referred to this as a "test of what we teach" approach. The advantage of a departmental exam is that the curriculum for a department is not going to be properly assessed if a national exam is used. Other popular assessment techniques at this level include capstone experiences and projects.

A variation of the departmental perspective is the disciplinary perspective, which reflects a kind of national consensus of what a field or discipline should include. The Graduate Record Exam (GRE) is an example of a test that has been utilized by a number of college departments as an assessment of graduating seniors. This approach has been criticized by some as a "teach to the test" view of assessment.

Another variation of the departmental perspective is the professional viewpoint, which attempts to assess the outcomes of a college education that are relevant to a profession or professional school. Assessment examples of this approach include the National Teachers Exam, Law School Aptitude Test (LSAT), Medical College Admission Test (MCAT), state bar exams, the National Board exam for medical school graduates, and the Uniform Certified Public Accountants (CPA) exam. These professional certification exams are developed with practicing professionals in the field with the objective of weeding out those who "don't get it" or "haven't learned it."

College or University Level

More than 20 years ago, David Webster identified the six most popular methods for evaluating effectiveness in higher education:

- Reputational ratings by peers or experts;
- Citation counts of faculty members in the institution;
- Faculty awards and honors—Fulbright or Guggenheim Fellowships;
- Student achievements after graduation;
- Scores of entering students on national exams—SAT, ACT; and
- Institutional resources—expenditures per student, size of library, size of student body (full-time equivalent), and so forth.[6]

Alexander Astin has suggested that it is possible to create a taxonomy of student outcomes by considering the type of outcome (cognitive or affective) with the type of data—psychological or behavioral—as noted in Table 4.1 (p. 40).[7] Cognitive outcomes have to do with knowledge and the use of higher order processes such as reasoning and logic. The affective outcomes have to do with the student's feelings, values, beliefs, attitudes, aspirations, self-concept, and social and interpersonal relationships.

Table 4.1. Taxonomy of Student Outcomes*

Type of Data	Type of Outcome	
	Cognitive	**Affective**
Psychological	Subject matter knowledge	Values
	Academic ability	Beliefs
	Critical thinking ability	Interests
	Basic learning skills	Attitudes
	Special aptitudes	Self-concept
	Academic achievement	Satisfaction with college
Behavioral	Degree attainment	Leadership
	Vocational achievement	Citizenship
	Awards or special recognition	Hobbies and avocations

*Adapted from Alexander W. Astin. *Assessment for Excellence: The Philosophy and Practice of Assessment and Evaluation in Higher Education.* New York: The American Council on Education, 1991, 45.

It is also important to recognize that participation in the college experience will have both short-term (while the student is still in college) and long-term effects on student development. Incorporating the time dimension into the above taxonomy of student outcomes results in an expanded taxonomy that helps illustrate the effects of time, as shown in Table 4.2.

Table 4.2 The Perspective of Time on Student Outcomes*

Type of Outcome	Type of Data	Short-Term (During College)	Long-Term (After College)
Cognitive	Behavioral	Completion of college (versus dropping out)	Award for outstanding job achievement
	Psychological	MCAT score	Score on medical licensing exam
Affective	Behavioral	Participation in student government	Involvement in local or national politics
	Psychological	Satisfaction with college	Job satisfaction

*Adapted from Alexander W. Astin. *Assessment for Excellence: The Philosophy and Practice of Assessment and Evaluation in Higher Education.* New York: The American Council on Education, 1991, 46.

More recently, some colleges and universities have developed core objectives or abilities that all students must master. These core objectives or activities then form the foundation for all assessment activities. For example, Alverno College[8] in Wisconsin has established eight abilities:

- *Communication*—learning to read, write, speak, and listen effectively using graphics, electronic media, computers, and quantified data.

- *Analysis*—thinking clearly and critically by fusing experience, reason, and training into considered judgment.

- *Problem solving*—Defining problems and identifying their causes using a range of abilities and resources to reach decisions and make recommendations.

- *Valuing*—Recognizing the existence of different value systems while holding strongly to one's own ethic.

- *Social interaction*—Knowing how to get things done in committees, task forces, team projects, and other group efforts.

- *Global perspective*—Acting with understanding of and respect for the economic, social, and biological interdependence of global life.

- *Effective citizenship*—Being involved and responsible in one's community.

- *Aesthetic engagement*—Engaging with various forms of art and in the artistic processes.

A similar approach has been taken by the Southeast Missouri State University[9] in Cape Girardeau, which has established four general educational core objectives:

- *To develop higher-order thinking and reasoning.* Students should be able to distinguish among opinions, facts, and inferences; to identify underlying or implicit assumptions; to make informed judgments; and to solve problems by applying evaluative standards.

- *To develop effective communication skills.* Students should be able to read and listen critically and to write and speak with thoughtfulness, clarity, coherence, and persuasiveness.

- *To manage information.* Students should be able to locate, organize, store, retrieve, evaluate, synthesize, and annotate information from print, electronic, and other sources in preparation for solving problems and making informed decisions.

- *To develop moral and ethical values.* Students should be able to make informed decisions through identifying personal values and the values of others and through understanding how such values develop. They should be able to analyze the ethical implications of choices made on the basis of these values.

Southeast Missouri has been assessing the core competencies across the undergraduate curriculum in a way that involves faculty and students; provides a formal feedback loop to students, faculty, and administrators; and is used to improve student learning. Southeast's assessment plan is linked to the mission, goals, and objectives of the institution for student learning and academic achievement, including learning in general education and in the major. Results from assessment activities have led to changes in curriculum, special projects intended to improve teaching and learning, and changes in advising procedures. And while assessment of academic programs is administered by departments, colleges, and schools, the position of director of planning and assessment was created to provide oversight and advice.

An Assessment Guide

Assessment requires consideration of three basic questions: (1) What should a student get out of any college? (2) What should a student get out of attending this college? and (3) What does a student actually receive from attending this college? Focusing on these questions in a systematic assessment program will foster increased clarity about the purposes of an undergraduate education.

Peggy Maki developed an assessment guide, represented in three segments, which is designed to assist an educational institution in conceptualizing a plan. The guide consists of three parts (see Figure 4.1A–C): Determining your institution's expectations; determining timing, identifying cohort(s), and assigning responsibility; and interpreting and sharing assessment results.[10] Decisions about *what* to assess are related to decisions *how* to assess. But first and foremost, it is important to determine *what* to assess.

A. State Expected Outcomes	B. Identify Where Expected Outcomes Are Addressed	C. Determine Methods and Criteria to Assess Outcomes	D. State Institution's or Program's Level of Expected Perfomance	E. Identify and Collect Baseline Information
For example:	*For example:*	*For example:*	*For example:*	*For example:*
Derive supportable inferences from statistical and other data	Courses	Tests	National exam numerical score	Standardized tests
	Programs	Asses writing skills	License exam score	Local tests
Analyze a social problem from interdisciplinary perspectives	Services	Analysis of a problem	Assessment of mathematical problem solving	Writing skills assessment
	Internships	Collaborative problem-solving project		Case study analysis
Evaluate proposed solutions to a community issue	Community service projects	Portfolio	Culminating project assessment	Portfolio
	Work experiences	Simulation	Assessment of writing samples	
	Independent studies	Focus group		

Figure 4.1A. Determining Your Institution's Expectations

A. Determine Whom You Will Assess

For example:

All students

Student cohorts, such as:
At risk students
Students with high SAT scores
Students entering college at 25+
International students

B. Establish a Schedule for Assessment

For example:

Upon graduation

At the end of a specific semester/quarter

Upon completion of a required set of courses

Upon completion of a specific number of credits

A number of years after graduation

C. Determine Who Will Analyze Results

For example:

Outside Evaluators:
Faculty at neighboring institutions
Employers
Alumni

Inside Evaluators:
Interdisciplinary team
Librarians
Assessment Committee
Writing center staff
Student Affairs staff

Figure 4.1B. Determining Timing, Identifying Cohorts, and Assigning Responsibility for Assessment

A. Interpret How Results Will Inform Teaching/Learning and Decision Making

For example:

Revise teaching styles, curricula, sequence of course

Create a more effective student orientation

Describe outcomes more effectively

Increase connections between in-class and out-of-class learning

Review institutional planning, decision making, and allocation of resources

B. Determine How and with Whom You Will Share Interpretations

For example:

An annual report of the Curriculum Committee

Annual report of the Assessment Committee

Departments systematically review assessment data

Periodic reviews by the planning & budgeting groups

Self-study reports in preparation for accreditation visits

Figure 4.1C. Interpreting and Sharing Assessment Results

Effective and useful assessment measures should be unambiguous and be linked to indicators of quality. Many institutional assessment plans focus on "student outcomes": aggregate statistics on groups of students using such measures as graduation rates and employment rates. The focus on student outcomes does not determine the impact of the college experience in the lives of the students.

"Student learning outcomes," on the other hand, encompass a wide range of student attributes and abilities, both cognitive and affective, which measure how the collegiate experience has supported their development as individuals.

Types of Measures

It is possible to separate assessment measures into two broad groups:

- *Direct measures* are performance based and focus on the actual work that students have produced. Possible direct measures are capstone experiences, portfolio assessment, standardized tests, certification and license exams, locally developed exams, essay exams that use multiple individuals to provide blind scoring, juried review of student performances and projects, and external evaluation of student performance in internships.

- *Indirect measures* could include surveys, exit interviews, retention and transfer rates, length of time to a degree, SAT and ACT test scores, graduate rates, and placement and acceptance data. Note that faculty/student ratios, curriculum review documents, accreditation reports, demographic data, and other administrative data are generally not acceptable measures of student outcomes. Some of these are input measures and some are a mix of measures.

Direct Measures

Direct measures often ask students to grapple with solving realistic and unstructured problems that typically have no "right" answer. Regardless of the method selected, the criteria being used for assessment should be in writing and very explicit.

The Capstone Experience

The capstone experience has been recognized as an effective means of providing students with an opportunity to integrate and reflect on what they have learned and experienced in a program. The capstone experience assists in addressing the "piecemeal approach" to the undergraduate program and provides a sense of closure and connection between courses.

The structure and content of the capstone experience is typically linked to the established educational goals and objectives of the department or program. The standards that will be used to evaluate student learning during and upon completion of the capstone experience must be clearly articulated to the students.

The capstone experience can be used by students to

- integrate and synthesize the field;
- extend the field;
- critique the field;
- apply the field;
- address issues raised in the introductory course, but at a higher level;
- explore key arguments in the field;
- make connections with general education;
- make specific comparisons with other fields;
- critically assess the field; and
- examine values and views of life.[11]

In some cases, interdisciplinary teams of faculty members and/or graduates of the program are used to rate the capstone experience and use a scoring rubric that has been developed and validated by the program faculty. Typical criteria for assessing a capstone experience include

- organization and development of the thesis statement;
- application of the theoretical/conceptual framework;
- empirical support of the thesis;
- bibliographic sources;
- format and style of presentation; and
- grammar, spelling, and other "mechanics" of writing.[12]

The Standardized Test

A variety of standardized tests have been used by some institutions for a direct assessment of their programs. The advantage of a standardized test is that the institution can compare itself against national norms and benchmark comparisons with peer institutions. Clearly the faculty of a program or department must ensure that the standardized test is going to fairly assess what has been taught to the students rather than using it simply because it is available.

Using a standardized test in a pre-test and post-test methodology will more accurately reflect the value added by the program. Among these standardized tests are the following:

- *Academic Profile Test.* This test includes material usually covered in courses taken during the first two years of college, the "core curriculum" or "general education requirements." It is intended for use by colleges and universities in assessing the outcomes of their general education programs to improve the quality of instruction and learning. More information is available at http://www.ets.org.

- *California Critical Thinking Skills Test.* The CCTST Total Score targets the strength or weakness of one's skill in making reflective, reasoned judgments about what to believe or what to do. The CCTST generates several scores relating to critical thinking. More information is available at http://www.insightassessment.com/test-cctst.html.

- *Collegiate Assessment of Academic Proficiency* (CAAP). This is the standardized, nationally normed assessment program from ACT that enables postsecondary institutions to *measure*, *evaluate*, and *enhance* the outcomes of their general education programs. More information is available at http://www.act.org/caap/.

- The *Behavioral Event Interview* (BEI) of the Student Potential Program, sponsored by the Council for Adult and Experiential Learning, consists of an intensive one-hour interview that elicits information about critical events in the student's life. The primary drawback with this approach is the labor-intensive nature of this exam—it takes a minimum of two hours to score the interview.

- *College BASE* is a criterion-referenced achievement test designed to assess student proficiency in English, mathematics, science, and social studies together with three cross-disciplinary cognitive competencies: strategic reasoning, interpretive reasoning, and adaptive reasoning. More information is available at http://arc.missouri.edu/CB/CBoutsideMO_InstInfo.htm.

- *Major Field Achievement Test.* The Major Field Tests are innovative undergraduate and MBA outcomes assessments designed to measure the basic knowledge and understanding achieved by students in a major field of study. Test results enable academic departments to better assess and refine curricula and gauge the progress of students compared to others in the program and those in similar programs at schools throughout the country. More information is available at http://www.ets.org.

- The *California Basic Education Skills Test* (CBEST) for teachers. The CBEST is designed to test basic reading, mathematics, and writing skills found to be important for the job of an educator; the test is not designed to measure the ability to teach those skills. More information is available at http://www.cbest.nesinc.com/.

- *Professional Assessment Examination for Beginning Teachers* (PRAXIS). The Praxis assessments provide tests and other services that some states use as part of their teaching licensing certification process. The *Praxis I* tests measure basic academic skills, the *Praxis II* tests measure general and subject-specific knowledge and teaching skills, and the *Praxis III* tests assess classroom performance. More information is available at www.ets.org/praxis.

- *Entering Student Needs Assessment Survey.* The purpose of this survey is to ask entering first-time freshmen for their best estimate of the amount of help they will require in specific skill areas over the course of their academic careers. More information is available at http://www.udel.edu/IR/reports/needs/index.html.

- *College Student Experiences Survey.* This survey asks students how they spent their time during their college careers—with friends, faculty, classes, and social events—as well as use of campus facilities, including the library and student center. More information is available at www.surveyconsole.com/college-student-experiences-questionnaire.html.

- *Collegiate Learning Assessment* (CLA). The Collegiate Learning Assessment begins with conceptions of collegiate quality that are based on improvements in student learning, with three key elements serving as the project's foundation: the institution, value added, and campus comparisons. The CLA uses the institution (rather than the individual student) as the primary unit of analysis. The CLA focuses on the value added provided by colleges and universities. This approach also allows for inter-institutional comparisons of overall value added. CLA results can be combined with institutional data to determine factors that promote student learning and growth. More information is available at http://www.cae.org/content/pro_collegiate.htm.

- Another group of instruments is designed to assess undergraduate admissions (the SAT and ACT) and for admission to graduate school and professional schools (GRE, LSAT, MCAT, and GMAT—Graduate Management Admission Test).

- *Withdrawing/Nonreturning Student Survey*. This survey provides an in-depth look at students' reasons for leaving college before completing a degree or certificate program. More information is available at http://www.act.org/ess/fouryear.html.

- *Alumni Outcomes Survey* assesses alumni's perceptions of an institution's impact on their personal and professional growth and development and provides a detailed employment and education history. More information is available at http://www.act.org/ess/fouryear.html.

- *ICT Literacy Test*. The ICT Literacy Assessment is a comprehensive test of information and communication technology proficiency that uses scenario-based tasks to measure both cognitive and technical skills. The assessment provides support for institutional ICT literacy initiatives, guides curricula innovations, informs articulation and progress standings, and assesses individual student proficiency. More information is available at www.ets.org.

- *SAILS Test*. Project SAILS is a standardized test of information literacy skills, based on ACRL Information Literacy Competency Standards for Higher Education. This Web-based tool allows libraries to document information literacy skill levels for groups of students and to pinpoint areas for improvement. More information is available at https://www.projectsails.org/sails/aboutSAILS.php?page=aboutSAILS.

- *Project MINES for Libraries*. Measuring the Impact of Networked Electronic Services (MINES) is an online transaction-based survey that collects data on the purpose of using electronic resources and the demographics of users. More information is available at http://www.arl.org/stats/newmeas/mines.html.

To assist in the instrument selection process, Dary Erwin, Elizabeth Jones, and Steve RiCharde have developed assessment sourcebooks that review a wide variety of commercially available instruments and evaluate them based on purpose, cost, types of scores, reliability, and validity.[13] Other guides that describe the available tests and other instruments include *The Mental Measurements Yearbook*[14] and *Tests in Print*.[15]

The disadvantages of the national standardized tests are that the tests are expensive and may not reflect the goals and objectives of a specific program or educational institution. Thus there is a role for the locally developed test.

The Locally Developed Test

A number of institutions have developed their own tests rather than relying on the standardized tests. This is most often done when the material being covered in a program is not similar to what the standardized test is attempting to assess. When carefully developed and validated, local tests will most likely produce more accurate information about their students' abilities and skills, knowledge, behaviors, and values than can be achieved by the standardized approach. However, few instructors and departments make the effort to validate local tests.

The Print-Based Portfolio

A number of institutions ask the student to prepare a print-based portfolio of his or her work for assessment. A portfolio is a structured, focused, and purposeful collection of student work. Clearly the student needs to ensure that the work included in the portfolio is representative of his or her best work. A systematic procedure should be in place to instruct the student in how to select materials for the portfolio. Faculty should develop a reliable rating rubric to score the contents of the print portfolio, as noted previously in the discussion regarding the capstone experience.

Some of the considerations that should be addressed prior to deciding to use a portfolio follow:

- What are the goals and objectives for the student creating the portfolio?
- What guidance will be given to assist a student in selecting materials to include?
- How and when will work be included in the portfolio?
- How will portfolios be reviewed, evaluated, and graded?
- Who will assess each portfolio?
- Will the student retain ownership of the portfolio?
- How will the portfolio be stored? How will access to the portfolio be controlled?

The advantages of the portfolio are that the goals and objectives for student learning have been articulated by the department, and the student has the opportunity to link the contents of the portfolio to these goals. Contributions to the portfolio typically reflect student learning and progress over the academic career. Students may be afforded the opportunity to reflect on their learning and how the courses and assignments have been linked to achieving educational goals.

However, among other problems with this assessment method, the assessment of print-based portfolios is labor intensive, and issues of determining a specific student's contribution to a team project must be carefully considered.

The Electronic Portfolio

A growing number of academic institutions are using the electronic portfolio as a measure of student learning. An electronic portfolio offers exciting possibilities for learning and assessment, since portfolios can

- *Feature multiple examples of work* reflecting a range of work, thus demonstrating the student's progress toward achieving educational goals and objectives;

- *Provide context rich evidence* allowing the student to set the stage for presenting his or her work;

- *Offer opportunities for selection and self-assessment* by demonstrating the student's ability to make choices based on criteria; and

- *Reflect development over time,* which enables those who are viewing the portfolio to better understand achievement over time.[16]

Portfolios offer students the opportunity for reflection, which is central to learning. Electronic portfolios can incorporate assessment into the educational process and facilitate learning for students, faculty, and institutions by strengthening the feedback loop. Since portfolios are albums rather than a single snapshot (the grade for a single test), they illustrate the process of learning. One disadvantage of the electronic portfolio is that the student must develop a basic set of technology skills to create and maintain the portfolio (which is a measure of how well a student can do this). The Rose-Hulman Institute of Technology has made extensive use of the electronic portfolio.[17]

A number of guides have been developed that address the range of issues associated with the creation, use, and maintenance of electronic portfolios.[18]

Indirect Measures

The intent of indirect measures is to provide assessment data that reflect the students' *perceptions* regarding the extent of and value of their learning experiences.

The Surveys

Those taking surveys to discover the perceived value of the collegiate experience include students, alumni, and employers. The principal challenge with this type of survey is that it yields self-report data of the opinions of how much was learned or how valuable the experience was.

Perhaps the most popular of the indirect surveys are those conducted with students, in particular graduating seniors, to discover their reactions and attitudes about what they experienced in both general education classes as well as courses in their major. Examples of these surveys include the Cooperative Institutional Research Program (CIRP) survey,[19] the Entering Student Survey (ESS), the ACT Student Opinion Survey (SOS),[20] and the College Outcomes Survey (COS).[21]

The National Survey of Student Engagement (NSSE) focuses on five learning-centered benchmarks of effective educational practice that research has linked to desired outcomes of the four-year college experience and thus are indicators of quality in undergraduate education. These five areas are level of academic challenge, student interaction with faculty members, active and collaborative learning, enriching educational experiences, and supportive campus environments.[22] A companion to the NSSE, called the Community College Survey of Student Engagement (CCSSE), is also available for use in two-year institutions.[23]

Locally developed surveys of alumni and employers are also very popular. Asking employers who are hiring the graduates of a college or university to assess the quality of their new employees is done frequently. Tracking the results of this survey over time allows the college or university to get a sense of how well its curriculum, its teaching, and the total academic experience are measuring up to the expectations of a broad set of employers while increasing stakeholder participation in the assessment process or institution. This is especially true for the trade and for-profit academic institutions. These latter organizations obviously place a high value on their ability to find good jobs for their graduates and to ensure that the graduates are well prepared to perform on the job.

While some businesses are satisfied with the technical skills developed by graduates within their major disciplines, many business leaders report that university graduates are deficient in several areas: written and oral communication skills, teamwork, and the capacity for lifelong learning.[24]

Studies

A college might engage in a series of studies to determine the persistence, retention, transfer, and graduation rates among its undergraduate students. Other studies might calculate the length of time it takes the average student to graduate. These types of studies are typically done to compare one institution with other peer institutions.

Some universities will prepare a follow-up study of their graduates in order to build a profile to their success in life after college. Such studies might determine the type of job career being pursued, the salary currently being earned, size of family, additional education and training received, and so forth.

Exit Interviews

Some institutions will ask a large sample of their graduating seniors to participate in either one-on-one exit interviews or a focus group to obtain their views on their educational experiences.

Assessment of Interpersonal Skills

Assessment of declarative knowledge measures focuses on cognitive-type learning to the exclusion of affective and skill-based learning. Increasingly, organizations are looking for individuals who have good interpersonal skills. As shown in Table 4.3, several methods can be used for assessment in this area.

Other Measures

Other indirect assessment methods include

- Retention and graduation statistics;
- Graduate student publications, fellowships, and post-doctorates;
- Placement in jobs or further schooling;
- Student perceptions of their own learning;
- Measures of the behaviors of faculty and students that research has shown to be linked to learning;
- Data on teaching practices or attitudes that research has shown to be linked to greater student learning; and
- Alumni surveys.

Assessment Example

The Indiana University Purdue University at Indianapolis (IUPUI) is developing a system of performance indicators to demonstrate the university's effectiveness in pursuing its mission. It is relying on a series of measures that reflect multiple strategic components. For example, the mission statement for "effective student learning" in the university has identified strategic components and performance measures, as shown in Table 4.4 (p. 56).

Table 4.3 Assessing Interpersonal Skills*

Measurement Technique	Administrative Cost	Relative Objectivity	What Is Being Measured?
Personality Inventories	Low	Low—self-report	Personality temperament—not interpersonal skills
Interviews	Moderate	Low to moderate—opportunity to view skills	Varied—may include communication skills, past behaviors, skill at relating to the interviewer
Peer Evaluations	Low	Moderate—classmates may have difficulty in providing constructive and unbiased feedback	Perceptions of behaviors and contributions toward group goals
360 Degree Feedback	High—significant data collection and analysis required	Moderate—classmates may have varied motives for providing accurate feedback	Multiple sources assessing behaviors in unstructured circumstances
Assessment Center	High—need to develop, administer, and provide feedback to students	High—need for trained, unbiased assessors to provide feedback	Perceptions of behavior in standardized and realistic work simulations

*Adapted from Willaim H. Bommer, Robert S. Rubin, and Lynn K. Bartels. Assessing the Unassesable: Interpersonal and Managerial Skills, in Kathryn Martell and Thomas Calderon, eds., *Assessment of Student Learning in Business Schools: Best Practices Each Step of the Way*. Tallahassee, FL: Association for Institutional Research, 2005, 106.

Table 4.4 IUPUI Performance Indicators for Effective Student Learning

Strategic Component	Performance Indicator
Access and support	Overall enrollment
	Quality of new students
	Diversity of new students
	Effectiveness of support services
Student proficiency	Grade performance
	Learning gains
Student progress	Retention rate
	Graduation rate
	Degree production
Career and professional development	Job outcomes of alumni
	Further education pursuits of alumni
	Continued learning opportunities
Experiential and community-based learning	Student participation
Quality of programs	Reputation, rankings, and ratings
	Faculty credentials
	Quality of learning environment

It is important to note that IUPUI has selected a number of strategic components and performance measures to reflect its progress toward the goal of improving the effectiveness of student learning. Clearly this university is just embarking on the assessment road, since the majority of these performance measures have little to do with the university's performance.

Tip! Another university that has developed a portfolio to present its commitment to assessment is the California State University at Sacramento. Its portfolio is available at www.csus.edu/portfolio.

Summary

The vast majority of colleges and universities are collecting student assessment data such as basic skills, progress to degree, and academic intentions. Yet only about a third of academic institutions assess students' higher-order learning skills, affective development, or professional skills.[25]

Recognizing that learning is multidimensional, it is important to utilize multiple assessment methods. No single method will accurately or fully assess all important student outcomes. A comprehensive assessment program should contain measures that are formative as well as summative, direct as well as indirect, and course-focused as well as institutional-focused.

Notes

1. Regional accrediting organizations for higher education include Middle States Commission on Higher Education(Philadelphia, PA. http://www.msache.org); New England Association of Schools and Colleges Commission on Institutions of Higher Education (Bedford, MA, http://www.neasc.org); New England Association of Schools and Colleges Commission on Technical and Career Institutions (Bedford, MA, http://www.neasc.org); North Central Association of Colleges and Schools, The Higher Learning Commission (Chicago, IL, http://www.ncahigherlearningcommission.org); Northwest Association of Schools and of Colleges and Universities Commission on Colleges and Universities (Redmond, WA, http://www.nwccu.org); Southern Association of Schools and Colleges Commission on Colleges (Decatur, GA, http://www.sacscoc.org); Western Association of Schools and Colleges, the Senior College Commission (Alameda, CA, http://www.wascweb.org); and Western Association of Schools and Colleges Accrediting Commission for Community and Junior Colleges (Novato, CA, http://www.accjc.org).

2. George D. Kuh, Jillian Kinzie, John H. Schuh, Elizabeth J. Whitt and Associates. *Student Success in College: Creating Conditions That Matter.* San Francisco: Jossey-Bass, 2005, 266.

3. Catherine Palomba and Trudy Banta. *Assessment Essentials: Planning, Implementing and Improving Assessment in Higher Education.* San Francisco: Jossey-Bass, 1999.

4. Quoted in Michael Scriven. Beyond Formative and Summative Evaluation, in M.W. McLaughlin and Ed C. Phillips, eds., *Evaluation and Education: A Quarter Century.* Chicago: University of Chicago Press, 1991, 169.

5. T. W. Banta and J. A. Schneider. Using Faculty-Developed Exit Examinations to Evaluate Academic Programs. *Journal of Higher Education*, 59 (1), 1988, 69–83.

6. David S. Webster. Methods of Assessing Quality. *Change*, October 1981, 20–24.

7. Alexander W. Astin. *Assessment for Excellence: The Philosophy and Practice of Assessment and Evaluation in Higher Education.* New York: The American Council on Education, 1991.

8. For more information, go to http://www.alverno.edu/about_alverno/ability_curriculum.html (accessed March 21, 2007).

9. For more information, go to http://cstl.semo.edu/gesc/status_reports/UMR42Block_Status_Rpt.htm (accessed March 21, 2007).

10. Peggy L. Maki. Developing an Assessment Plan to Learn about Student Learning. *The Journal of Academic Librarianship*, 28 (1/2), 2002, 8–13.

11. Theodore C. Wagenaar. The Capstone Course. *Teaching Sociology*, 21 (3), July 1993, 209–14.

12. Robert J. Durel. The Capstone Course: A Rite of Passage. *Teaching Sociology*, 21 (3), July 1993, 223–25

13. T. Dary Erwin. *The NPEC Sourcebook on Assessment: Volume 1. Definitions and Assessment Methods for Critical Thinking, Problem Solving, and Writing.* Washington, DC: National Postsecondary Education Cooperative and the National Center for Education Statistics, 2000; T. Dary Erwin. *The NPEC Sourcebook on Assessment: Volume II. Selected Institutions Utilizing Assessment Results.* Washington, DC: National Postsecondary Education Cooperative and the National Center for Education Statistics, 2000; and Elizabeth A. Jones and Steve RiCharde. *Assessment Sourcebook: A Review of Instruments to Assess Communication, Teamwork, Leadership, Quantitative Reasoning, and Information Literacy Outcomes.* Washington, DC: U.S. Department of Education, The National Center for Education Statistics and the National Postsecondary Education Cooperative, 2004.

14. Robert A. Spies, Barbara S. Plake, and Linda L. Murphy. *The Sixteenth Mental Measurements Yearbook.* Lincoln: University of Nebraska Press, 2005.

15. Linda L. Murphy and Barbara S. Blake, eds. *Tests in Print.* Lincoln: University of Nebraska Press, 2006.

16. Liz Hamp-Lyons and William Condon. *Assessing the Portfolio: Principles for Practice, Theory and Research.* Creskill, NJ: Hampton Press, 1998.

17. The RosE Portfolio is an online, digital system developed at Rose-Hulman Institute of Technology. It is designed to allow students, faculty, and administrators to archive, assess, and evaluate student work for the purpose of class, department, program, and institutional assessment. For more information, go to http://www.rose-hulman.edu/REPS/ (accessed March 21, 2007).

18. See, for example, Marilyn Heath. *Electronic Portfolios: A Guide to Professional Development and Assessment.* Worthington, OH: Linworth Publishing, 2004; and Barbara Cambridge, ed. *Electronic Portfolios: Emerging Practices in Student, Faculty, an Institutional Learning.* Washington, DC: American Association of Higher Education, 2001.

19. For more information, go to http://www.gseis.ucla.edu/heri/cirp.html (accessed March 21, 2007).

20. For more information, got to http://www.act.org/ess/fouryear.html (accessed March 21, 2007).

21. For more information, go to http://www.act.org/ess/fouryear.html (accessed March 21, 2007).

22. Cecilia L. Lopez. Assessment of Student Learning: Challenges and Strategies. *The Journal of Academic Librarianship*, 28 (6), November 2002, 356–67.

23. For more information, go to http://www.ccsse.org/ (accessed March 21, 2007).

24. Diana G. Oblinger and Anne-Lee Verville. *What Business Wants from Higher Education.* Phoenix: American Council on Education, Oryx Press, 1998; and Nancy P. Goldschmidt. Lessons Learned from Surveying Employers. *Assessment Update*, 17 (4), July–August 2005, 1–3, 13.

25. Marvin Lazerson, Ursula Wagener, and Nichole Shumanis. What Makes a Revolution? Teaching and Learning in Higher Education. *Change*, 32 (3), 2000, 12–19.

Chapter

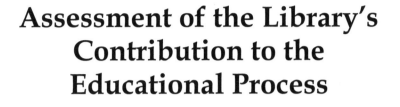

Assessment of the Library's Contribution to the Educational Process

Historically, academic libraries have focused the majority of their attention on the library's collection and its organization. This collection focus is reflected in the annual rankings of the Association of Research Libraries, which are based on the size of the library's collection, budget, staffing levels, and several other factors. While the college and university library has been generally regarded as a potent educational force, its strength today is generally described using measures that reflect "bricks, bytes, and books."

Attempting to assess the library's contribution to the academic success of college and university students is problematic due to a wide variety of factors that influence academic success, as noted in previous chapters of this book, as well as to the reluctance of the profession to carefully examine the role of the library.

Use of the Library

Ideally, the college or university library would be assessed by identifying the extent to which students use it and the degree to which such use relates to academic growth and success. However, use does not necessarily have a causal link to learning and academic success. Unfortunately few studies have examined the possible link between use and academic growth. Further, such studies are complicated by several factors:

- Circulation records do not, in most cases, include the use of materials in the library by students and faculty that are not borrowed.

- The analysis does not reflect use of journals (photocopies made or articles downloaded).

- Studies based on self-reported activity in surveys and interviews rely on an accurate memory (not always present).

- Use of diaries or logs typically has very small sample sizes.

- Use of a citation analysis methodology does not take into account the items read or used in some way but not cited (this latter methodology is perhaps more appropriate for identifying use by graduate students and faculty).

Physical Resources

W. E. Troutt, who examined accreditation documents to discover the correlates of educational quality and college impact, found that there was no relationship between differences in library resources and student achievement.[1] A related study, which analyzed the number of library books per student and library size and undergraduates' scores on the Graduate Record Examination (GRE), found no statistically significant correlations between an institution's academic library resources and undergraduates' educational outcomes.[2]

Another study examined the relationship between the number of books in the library and the number of books in the library per student and the student scores on the GRE. After controlling for the students' background characteristics, Astin found only a weak positive correlation between library size and scores on the GRE.[3] An additional study also found a weak correlation between undergraduates' scores on both the GRE and the Scholastic Aptitude Test (SAT) and the number of books in the library and the number of library books per student.[4] Implicit in these studies of the size of the library, sometimes called *resource allocation analysis,* was the assumption that "if you have it, they will use it." Also, it is likely that the larger universities have excellent reputations that help attract the brightest students.

An analysis of the factors that influenced library use found that library use being required in the course, the library being discussed in class, and library orientation accounted for about one-third of all library use. Perceptions of library services, positive or negative, accounted for about 10 percent of use.[5] Another study examined the factors that influenced undergraduates' academic library use and found that levels of high school library use, student-faculty interactions, and active learning and engaged writing activities predicted levels of library use. Those undergraduates with higher levels of library use had higher self-reported and objective critical thinking scores.[6] A further study found only weak support for the use of materials in the stacks of a library and better grades for students majoring in history and sociology.[7]

An additional inquiry examined student characteristics and undergraduate library use and found that five variables influenced library use: hours spent on campus, credit hour enrollment, gender (male), grade point average, and academic major.[8] Similar results were noted in a study by Ethelene Whitmire, which observed that the more students studied the more they used the library.[9] However, a different analysis found that the amount of time spent in the library was not associated with academic success, and a positive correlation was observed between academic achievement and the use of different library resources and services.[10]

Law students who received honors upon graduation were more active book borrowers than students who did not graduate with honors.[11] A study conducted at the University of Delaware investigated the long-term borrowing of books from the general collection. The majority of students did not borrow any materials from the library—the percentage of students who did not borrow any materials declined somewhat from the freshman through the senior year. While students who did borrow materials were more likely to stay in school, the analysis revealed that the correlation was not statistically significant. In summary, it was found that the university's general collection was not widely used by undergraduates, and when it was used did not have a significant relationship to academic achievement.[12]

One study examined the use of the library and the dropout rate (sometimes called persistence). Lloyd Kramer and Martha Kramer found a statistically significant correlation between library use (as evidenced by circulation records) and persistence among college freshmen at California State Polytechnic College, Pomona. Forty-three percent of library nonusers dropped out within the first year, while only 26 percent of library users dropped out. In addition, users of the library had a slightly better grade point average (the correlation was statistically significant). Yet 65 percent of the freshmen borrowed no materials from the library.[13]

At Eastern Illinois University, it was found that about two-thirds of students borrowed no materials from the library. Yet a direct correlation was noted between the student's grade point average and the number of items borrowed from the library, indicating that more of the better students used the library.[14] In addition, very little support was found between usage of libraries and academic performance, but a link between extensive use of library catalogs and high academic performance was found.[15]

Another survey found that the library collection is deemed by many undergraduate students, to be superfluous to their educational program and found no correlation between use of the collection and academic achievement. Furthermore, no predictions could be made about library use based on a student's discipline or field of study.[16] A longitudinal analysis of faculty who used library information-seeking assignments found that such assignments are volatile due to turnover, use of adjuncts versus full-time faculty, as well as individual faculty preferences changing from year to year.[17] A study conducted at Penn State University found that only 8 percent of courses required much library use (students needed to gather information independently for a term paper), while nearly two-thirds of courses required no library use.[18]

Liberal arts college students' experiences with the library (more frequently asking librarians for assistance and using the library Web site to obtain resources for their academic work) are strongly correlated with working with a faculty member on research or discussing papers—perhaps because the library is in close proximity to where students live (on-campus student housing).[19]

James Self examined the use of reserve materials and students' grades in a variety of courses at the University of Virginia. Almost half of the 8,454 students included in the analysis did not use any reserve materials. While students with higher use of reserve materials tended to have higher grades, the statistical correlation was not significant and thus, use of reserve materials is not useful as a predictor of an individual's grade.[20] And undergraduates as a group requested materials though OhioLink at a disproportionately lower rate than either graduate students or faculty.[21]

A summary of the research studies discussed above is in Table 5.1.

Electronic Resources

Providing further complexity and confusion to the understanding of the impact of the library in the lives of college students are those students who avail themselves of the opportunity to take classes using the Internet, sometimes referred to as distance learning or distance education. One study that examined undergraduate students who took Internet-based courses found that they rely primarily on Internet sites and the materials provided by instructors through the tool used to provide the electronic course (Blackboard or WebCT) rather than using the electronic resources provided by the library.[22]

Carol Tenopir prepared an analysis concerning the use and users of electronic library resources.[23] She noted that the heaviest use of electronic resources is for research, followed by preparing for teaching and gaining current awareness. Graduate students are the heaviest and most cyclical users of electronic journals. Faculty members and professionals will use electronic journals if they are convenient, relevant, and time saving and support their natural work patterns. Peer-reviewed journals considered to be core to a researcher's work will be sought regardless of convenience. At the University of Washington, use of the physical library has declined while use of electronic resources has increased.[24]

A multiplicity of methods must be employed to gain a better understanding of who the remote users are, what users actually do, and why they do what they do. MINES for Libraries (Measuring the Impact of Networked Electronic Services) developed a Web-based survey of users of electronic resources. Brinley Franklin found that remote usage significantly exceeds in-library usage of electronic resources, sometimes by as much as four to one. Researchers depend more on electronic resources than on traditional print journals, and patterns of use vary by academic discipline.[25]

Table 5.1 Summary of Physical Resources Studies

Supportive	No Support
Astin (1968) Weak correlation between number of books/student (FTE) and GRE scores [669]	Nichols (1964) Library size and GRE scores showed no correlation
Rock et al. (1970) Weak support for number of library books/student (FTE) and GRE scores	Troutt (1979) No link between library resources and student achievement
De Jager (1997) Weak support for use of library materials and better grades [240]	
Whitmire (2001) Students who studied more used library resources more frequently [643]	Wells (1995) No link between time spent in the library and academic success [251]
Donovan (1996) More active book borrowers received higher grades	Lane (1966) No correlation between borrowing materials and academic success
Kramer and Kramer (1968) Library users more likely to stay in school [742]	Kramer and Kramer (1968) Most freshmen borrowed no materials
Barkey (1965) Link between items borrowed and student's GPA	Hiscock (1986) No support for use of the library and academic performance [192]
	Mays (1986) No link between use of the collection and academic achievement [465]
	Self (1987) No support for use of reserve materials and academic success [8,454]
	Schulz (2001) Undergraduates do not request materials from other libraries in proportion to their relative numbers [300]

The numbers in brackets are the sample sizes.

A survey of students at the University of Maryland found that remote access to full-text materials as well as citation and abstract databases is the most important service offered by the library.[26] While moving to electronic subscriptions can save the library money,[27] none of the surveys or other assessment methods have yet to tell the library why users select certain resources, or what value results from the resources provided by the library—value to the user and to the institution.

A study at Glasgow Caledonia University found that the highest retention and progression rate among students was among those with the highest rates of using electronic resources, especially electronic journals. Correspondingly, those students with the lowest use of electronic resources had the highest drop-out rates.[28]

In addition, some faculty members have found that the lack of availability of journal articles is a substantial problem and that "the process of locating information in academic journal literature is tedious and often hit or miss and the act of physically searching through hard-copy collections is much too time-consuming and onerous."[29]

One innovative approach builds on the studies conducted by Donald King and his colleagues starting in 1977. It asks faculty, researchers, and students about the time they spend reading and use of the print and electronic journal collections maintained by the library. A recent study at the University of Pittsburgh found that *if* the library's journal collection—physical and electronic—were not available, faculty would spend an additional 250,000 hours and some $2.1 million to use alternative sources to locate the desired articles.[30] Don King and his colleagues used a contingent valuation methodology, which asks survey respondents how much time and money they would spend to obtain the information they currently receive from the library's journal collection if the library collection were unavailable. Further analysis suggested that the total value of the library's journal collection to the university is $13.48 million less the costs for creating and maintaining the collection ($3.43 million), for a net value of $11.61 million. In other words, if there were no university library journal collection, it would cost the university 4.38 times the cost of the current library collection in faculty time and other expenditures for the same amount of research and information gathering to be carried out.

A summary of the research related to electronic resources is shown in Table 5.2.

Table 5.2 Summary of Electronic Resources Studies

Supportive	No Support
Hiller (2002) Use of the physical library has declined, while use of electronic resources has increased	Van Scoyco and Cason (2006) Students prefer Internet-based resources rather than library-provided resources [884]
Tenopir (2003) Electronic resources will be used if they are convenient, relevant, and time saving	
Kelly and Orr (2003) Access to electronic resources is the most important library service [2,713]	
Franklin and Plum (2006) Remote use of electronic resources greatly exceeds in-library use of these resources	
King et al. (2004) If no library journal collection existed, it would cost the university 4.38 times the cost of the current library journal collection to get the information needed [379]	

The numbers in brackets are the sample sizes.

Library as Employer

Several colleges made an interesting discovery when they found that the library work-study students had higher retention and graduation rates than their counterparts.[31] Stanley Wilder suggested that the possible "natural advantages of a library job" include the following:

- The library is demystified and thus the work-study student may have a positive predisposition for further use of its resources.
- Students are placed in an environment with good academic role models.
- Materials that will have value in completing course work are more readily apparent.[32]

Examining the relatively consistent findings of all of these studies, it is possible to come to the following conclusions:

- There is no clear evidence that library use is linked to learning or academic success.

- A considerable proportion of all undergraduate students borrow no materials from the library.
- A small proportion of students (10 to 15 percent) are responsible for a majority of borrowed materials.
- Assigned readings and course-related readings (reserves) account for the majority of circulation in most undergraduate libraries.
- The amount of borrowing varies by discipline or field of study.
- Borrowing by undergraduates increases by class rank—it is lowest among freshmen and highest among seniors.
- A few courses on a campus will generate the majority of library use.
- The studies do not control for student abilities and typically rely on a single measure of use and success.
- Studies that rely on self-evaluation of success may not be an accurate assessment of library skills.
- The correlation between library use and academic achievement is weak at best.

Evaluation of Library Instruction Programs

> *Carefully targeted, thoroughly prepared, well-presented, properly evaluated user education will be expensive indeed. We might remember S.R. Ranganathan's Fourth Law of Library Science: Save the Time of the Reader. This is more important than the Principle of Cost Effectiveness: Save the Time of the Librarian.*
>
> —Tom Eadie[33]

For a considerable period of time, academic libraries have been offering and providing bibliographic instruction, sometimes called library research instruction, under one guise or another. It is interesting to note that little effort is expended by libraries in reducing the complexity that leads to the need for bibliographic instruction.

In 1990 the Middle States Association Commission on Higher Education held that the centrality of a library/learning resources center in the educational mission of an institution deserves more than rhetoric and must be supported by more than lip service. An active and continuous program of bibliographic instruction is essential to realize this goal. . . . Nothing else matters much if the resources are not used.[34]

Since most libraries are not equipped with the budget or staff to provide bibliographic instruction for all entering students, assuming such instruction was mandated, an approach has been taken to integrate such bibliographic instructional concepts into freshmen-level courses. In the best of all worlds, the content would be cooperatively designed by a librarian and the course instructor.

Bibliographic instruction assessment efforts seem to fall into four categories: opinion surveys, knowledge testing, observing actual library use, and student persistence.[35] These categories are used to structure this overview.

Opinion Surveys

According to Richard Werking, what bibliographic instruction evaluation has been done has not been meaningful.[36] Typically the evaluations focused on user satisfaction rather than the development of learning competencies and other outcomes.[37] Aside from having difficultly identifying the benefits of instruction, the instruments that were used (surveys and skill tests) often lacked validity and reliability—it was not safe to rely on the results since the responses might not be linked to the question being asked or the skill being assessed.[38] Despite their popularity, the primary drawbacks with opinion surveys were that the questions often reflected the biases of the instrument's developers and the data generated did not measure the effectiveness of the instruction within the institution's context. In addition, the self-reported data can lead to validity problems.

One study that tracked results over a six-year period found little relationship between students' demographics, previous library instruction, or prior use of library resources and how they evaluated library instruction.[39]

Knowledge Testing

One study used an advanced statistical methodology (multiple regression techniques) to evaluate long-term library skills retention and their impact on students who took a library skills course. While the students who actively used the skills after the course had the best skills retention (no surprise there), the study found no significant relationship between library skills retention and SAT scores or eventual grade point averages.[40] However, the use of a Library Orientation Test did appear to forecast academic success in terms of grade point average in a sample of 81 students, a very small sample indeed.[41] Another study found no significant correlation between a library information competency class and the student's GPA.[42]

Self-assessment imposes serious methodological problems since it is often not reliable or valid. For example, 90 percent of students rated their library skills as adequate, but in a test of competencies, only 53 percent proved "minimally competent."[43]

Use of a pre-test and post-test methodology has the potential for more accurately understanding the knowledge transfer as the result of completing a class. One study using this approach with a sample of 404 students found no difference between pre- and post-test results.[44] Another study with a larger sample of 1,197 students found that the library class measurably improved the participants' library skills.[45] However, if the same instrument is used for the pre- and post-test, reported gains are suspect since students will likely remember questions and naturally improve their scores.

Another study assessed the quality of term papers prepared by students and tracked the long-range course completion rates of students. The students who completed a library orientation course were found to have written better papers and had higher course completion rates when compared to students who did not take the orientation class.[46] Similar findings were also noted in earlier studies.[47] Providing a contrary point of view, another analysis found that a library instruction program made little difference in the types of materials students chose for their research papers.[48] In addition, focusing on the style of the citations, the total number of citations, and variety of citations is a library-centric view of the world. It is much more important to determine the degree to which the instruction helped the students write better papers and achieve better grades, among other possible outcomes.

A more recent study found that there were statistically significant differences in citation use (use of more scholarly resources and the number of incomplete citations) and the grade received in the course for students who took a library course than those students who did not take the class.[49] A methodological problem associated with term paper analysis is that other variables, such as assistance from a reference librarian or friend, may interfere with the results.

Another study found significant differences between those who completed a bibliographic instruction class and a control group who did not attend the class. Bibliographic instruction class attendees had higher grade point averages and a higher persistence rate, yet there was no difference in graduation rates.[50] A three-year study determined that library use instruction is much more highly correlated with skill possession than either inherent intellectual ability or academic diligence.[51]

Donald Barclay suggested that the dearth of quality evaluations of library instructional classes was the result of limited institutional support, time constraints, and the difficulty of developing an effective evaluation process.[52] Barclay's solution was to "set [our] sights lower and do the best evaluation [we] can with what [we] have."[53] Rather than suggesting use of sloppy research, Barclay went on to recommend use of data, albeit less than perfect, which is better than using either no data or the soft data based on anecdotal observations and/or student satisfaction surveys. Such an approach was followed at The Citadel library, which found that use of the library increased for students taking the bibliographic instruction class, as evidenced by pre-test and post-test scores.[54]

A Johns Hopkins University study compared baseline measures of freshman library skills to upper-class students' skills and concluded that exposure to a library does not necessarily improve those skills, nor do students learn good library skills on their own.[55]

A quantitative analysis of student bibliographies submitted for courses in undergraduate institutions around Philadelphia found use of few electronic sources and no relationship between instruction in the use of electronic resources and increased usage of these sources.[56] A further study evaluated students taking a bibliographic instruction course and found that the students would obtain no greater bibliographical skills than those who did not take the course.[57]

> *A fact that must be considered, then, is that to an extraordinary degree the primary literature indexes itself, and does so with greater comprehensiveness, better analytics, and greater precision than does the secondary literature. Footnotes are, after all, the traditional medium whereby scholars communicate with each other directly. That is their purpose.*
> —Stephen K. Stoan[58]

A summary of these studies is shown in Table 5.3 (p. 72).

Actual Library Use

At Earlham College, bibliographic instruction was integrated into the course offerings of a majority of classes. It was found that the average graduate used the library in 54 percent of his or her courses (bibliographic instruction was included in about 37 percent of the courses). Unfortunately, no analysis was made to compare college graduates to dropouts and their use (or nonuse) of the library.[59]

Student Retention Rates (Persistence)

Interestingly, several studies have noted a positive correlation between a freshman orientation course and student persistence and strengthened academic performance. One analysis examined data that covered a 15-year period and found that students who participated in the orientation class had higher sophomore return rates and graduation rates despite the fact that many were less prepared academically than their nonparticipant counterparts.[60]

Table 5.3 Summary of Library Instruction Program Studies

Supportive	No Support
Opinion Surveys	
	Werking (1980) What bibliographic instruction has been done is not meaningful
	Eadie (1982) Validity and reliability problems with locally developed instruments
	Landrum and Muench (1994) Surveys often reflect the biases of librarians who develop the instruments
	Moore-Jansen (1997) No link between instruction and library use and opinions [403]
Knowledge Testing	
Corlett (1974) Library orientation class was linked to improved GPA scores [81]	Hardesty et al. (1982) No correlation between library skills retention and SAT or GPA scores [162]
	Moore et al. (2002) Library skills class is not linked to GPA scores
	Ware et al. (1986) Self-assessment of skills not linked to reality
	Colborn and Cordell (1998) Pre- and post-test method reveal no improvement in library skills [404]
Breivik (1977) Library orientation course resulted in better term papers	Emmons and Martin (2002) Library use instruction made little difference in type of materials selected for a term paper [250]
King and Ory; Dykeman and King (1983); Wilson (1986) Library skills class linked to better term papers	Malone and Videon (1997) Instruction does not lead to increased use of electronic sources in term papers [291]
Selegean et al (1983) Bibliographic instruction resulted in higher GPA scores [512]	Eyman and Nunley (1977) Library skills course does lead to improved bibliographic skills
Carter (2002) Bibliographic instruction class resulted in increased use of the library	
Wang (2006) Library instruction course resulted in more scholarly citations and better grades [120 papers, 836 citations]	

Numbers in square brackets are the sample sizes.

A similar study found that freshman orientation course participant grades were higher, the students reported increased use of university resources such as the library and writing services, and their overall retention rate was higher than their counterparts'.[61] Freshman orientation courses are cost-effective, given that they generate revenue due to increased student retention and thus offset the costs of the orientation class.[62]

Despite the studies noted here, the vast majority of libraries have done little or no evaluation of bibliographic instruction even though it is considered to be a "good thing."

> Bibliographic instruction seems to be perceived by many librarians simply as a self-evident social good, not needing an extensive rationale or empirical evidence to substantiate its effectiveness or even to support the need for it. Much of the literature of bibliographic instruction resembles a dialectic with the antithesis missing.[63]

In summarizing the plethora of articles reporting studies about library bibliographic instruction, a decidedly mixed picture emerges:

- The vast majority of new students who enter the college environment each year do not avail themselves of the opportunity to attend a library skills or bibliographic instruction class, provided such a class is offered.

- A majority of collegiate courses do not have a bibliographic instruction component that is integrated into the course content.

- A fair amount of the research focuses on opinion surveys and pre-test and post-test knowledge and library skill improvements, which do not evaluate student learning.

- Improvement in basic library skills is the means and not the end, and yet the former is the focus of most bibliographic instruction evaluation efforts.

- Few studies reported a link between bibliographic instruction and increased use of the library resources and services.

- Even fewer studies have focused on the link between bibliographic instruction and doing better academically (however this might be measured).

Evaluation of Information Literacy Programs

Before the various studies of information literacy are reviewed, the topic of critical thinking will be considered. Critical thinking is closely related to information literacy and can be defined as the ability to "interpret, evaluate, and make informed decisions about the adequacy of arguments, data, and conclusions."[64] One popular standardized test that is often used to assess critical thinking is the Watson-Glaser Critical Thinking Appraisal Test.[65]

One study was conducted to determine the relationship between an institution's academic library resources and services and undergraduates' library use and self-reported gains in critical thinking. Ethelene Whitmire found that the library's resources were related to self-reported gains in critical thinking for undergraduates attending research universities. Interestingly, she also found that academic library services were negatively related to undergraduates' use of the library. Undergraduates who were involved in more interactions with their faculty, engaged in more writing activities, and active participants in the classroom reported more library use. In addition, full-time students reported more library use than part-time students.[66]

In a related analysis, Whitmire noted that upperclassmen and students with better grades, students engaged in more focused library activities (compared to routine library use), and students actively participating in course learning and making conscientious revisions of their writings reported gains in their critical thinking.[67] Yet Whitmire also found that libraries with large numbers of bibliographic instruction participants and libraries with more service hours and greater utilization of document delivery and interlibrary loan services reported that fewer undergraduates used the library. Confounding the picture even further, Patrick Terenzini and others found negative relationships between library experiences and critical thinking scores.[68]

Starting late in the 1980s, Patricia Breivik and others presented the idea of information literacy, suggesting that it was an essential skill in lifelong learning.[69] These individuals believed that integration of information literacy into curricula serves as a major goal for the future success of academic libraries. While bibliographic instruction tends to focus on the organization of the library and its physical collections, the use of primary reference sources, and how to search the library catalog more effectively, information literacy focuses on the skills needed to handle and manipulate information in an online and Internet era.

Undergraduate students from high schools with library media teachers are more familiar with basic library use concepts, fundamental ideas of how information is organized and made accessible, and how to use online catalogs to advantage than are students from high schools without librarians. The students with good information literacy skills coming from high schools with librarians received better grades than students who attended schools without librarians.[70]

Academic librarians have turned to the concept of information literacy as a way to designate the importance of understanding how information is organized, how to find appropriate information resources, and how to assess information that is encountered during the search process. Unfortunately, "there is a temptation for students to settle for information that meets the 'three Fs' requirement: first, fastest, and full text."[71]

In general, information literacy involves recognizing a need for information, identifying what is needed, evaluating and organizing information, and learning to use it effectively. While acknowledging that developing information literacy skills will be important throughout the lives of undergraduate and graduate students, the issues of how to impart and assess those skills are very similar to those encountered by librarians when they were evaluating bibliographic instruction.

The Information Literacy Competency Standards for Higher Education, developed by the Association of College & Research Libraries (ACRL), state:

> Information literacy forms the basis for lifelong learning. It is common to all disciplines, to all learning environments, and to all levels of education. It enables learners to master content and extend their investigations, become more self-directed, and assume greater control over their own learning. An information literate individual is able to:
>
> - Determine the extent of information needed
>
> - Access the needed information effectively and efficiently
>
> - Evaluate information and its sources critically
>
> - Incorporate selected information into one's knowledge base
>
> - Use information effectively to accomplish a specific purpose
>
> - Understand the economic, legal, and social issues surrounding the use of information, and access and use information ethically and legally.[72]

Teaching information literacy skills is generally viewed as affecting student outcomes, since these skills support such educational outcomes as critical thinking, problem solving, and lifelong learning. Unfortunately this view is an assumption that is yet to be proven in a series of studies that can be replicated.

The majority of the information literacy literature focuses on three topics: opinion/satisfaction surveys, testing of skills by the participants of the information literacy courses, and actual information-seeking behavior. The Information Literacy Test, developed by the Educational Testing Service, was administered to 3,000 college students from 44 institutions and found that only 13 percent were deemed information literate.[73]

Opinion Surveys

Often this literature suggests that improvements should be made to teaching methods and modes of delivery of the information literacy content. For example, one study found that students of color, students satisfied with campus library facilities, and students engaged in interactions with faculty self-reported greatest satisfaction with their information literacy skills.[74]

Skills Testing

Another study used testing to gauge gains in information literacy as well obtaining the perspectives of librarians involved in instruction and of the students who claimed "success" but did not use an independent means to verify improved student grades.[75]

One evaluation of a curriculum-integrated information literacy program for undergraduate students showed that the participation had little or no long-term impact on students' searching skills.[76] Another study found that the differences between those who had attended library information literacy education sessions and those who had not were not that great.[77]

A study assessing information literacy at the University of California, Berkeley, found that students think they know more about accessing information and conducting library research than they are able to demonstrate when put to the test.[78] A different study found that students had difficulties defining a problem, determining where to go for information (that is, which sources to use), developing an effective search strategy, finding material in the library, and developing insights.[79]

Challenges arise when a library attempts to use a pre-test and post-test method of assessment. Locally developed questions are often not subjected to rigorous analysis to screen out use of jargon, or the answer might be indicated in another item. If the pre-test scores are high, there is very little room to differentiate the impact of the training from incidental changes, including test/retest effects.[80]

One recent study of students at Southeastern Louisiana University found that students who participated in an information literacy class had improved confidence levels in using the library yet failed to improve their pre-test to post-test performance on content questions.[81] Between 35 and 81 percent of the test participants received poor or failing scores. Similar disappointing findings were found in a study at Johns Hopkins University[82] and Indiana University, South Bend.[83]

Project SAILS (Standardized Assessment of Information Literacy Skills) is a Web-based, multiple-choice knowledge test targeting a variety of information literacy skills. A number of academic libraries have administered the test and, in general, the findings suggest that students' information literacy seems to improve throughout their academic careers due to their participation in an information literacy class.[84]

Observed Behavior

One study found that while students' learning is influenced by their previous experiences, they will engage with information literacy programs only to the extent that they perceive professors and instructors require them to do so.[85] Other studies have raised serious questions about students' abilities to seek and use information.[86]

Clearly the ready availability of a wide range of Internet-based resources (some of dubious quality and value) is having an impact on academic libraries. The well-publicized decline in ARL reference statistics is one handy indicator. One study of student searching behavior shows that commercial Internet search engines dominate students' information-seeking strategies. Some 45 percent of students use Google as their primary access method when attempting to locate information, while only 10 percent rely on the university library online catalog.[87] A companion survey, sponsored by the Pew Trust, found that 55 percent of college students completely agree that Google provides worthwhile information, compared with only 31 percent for library databases. In addition, Internet-based search engines are the first choice for research for 80 percent of the respondents; the online library for only 6 percent. Further, the respondents indicated that they see little difference between Internet resources and library-provided electronic databases.[88]

The OCLC survey indicates that search engines are used most often to begin information searches (89 percent), while a library Web site is selected by just 2 percent of college students.[89] The survey also found that college students favor libraries as a place to study, get free Internet access, and obtain materials, while they favor bookstores as coffee shops, to find current materials, and for meeting their friends.

An analysis of over 300,000 student respondents to the College Student Experiences Survey over a 19-year period found that library experiences do not seem to directly contribute to gains in information literacy, to what students gain overall from college, or to student satisfaction.[90]

Table 5.4 (p. 78) is a summary of the studies related to information literacy.

James Marcum has asked whether "information" is the appropriate literacy. He has suggested that other "literacies" deserve some consideration and are, perhaps, better suited for a student's long-term success in the job marketplace. Among the possible literacies vying for supremacy are visual literacy, technological literacy, computer-mediated communication literacy, computational literacy, and knowledge media literacy.[91] Perhaps literacy is not the appropriate focus, but rather possibly academic libraries should be concentrating on competencies, fluency, or expertise.

All of this suggests that librarians need to reconsider what students need to be taught and how librarians contribute to the student learning process. Implicit in this reconsideration is the need to focus library efforts on the outcomes of information literacy rather than on ways to improve the process of imparting skills or assessing the satisfaction levels of students who complete an information literacy course.

Table 5.4 Summary of Information Literacy Studies

Supportive	No Support
Smalley (2004) High school students with good information literacy skills received better grades than students who attended high schools without librarians [506]	Whitmire (1998) Libraries with large numbers of bibliographic instruction students report that few undergraduates used the library [18,157]
Skills Testing	
Julien and Boon (2004) Claimed gains in information literacy but no testing [28]	Brewer (1999) Information literacy program had no impact on students' searching skills
	Rabine and Cardwell (2000) Few differences between those who attended an information literacy class and those who did not [414]
	Maughan (2001) Students' perceptions of their skills are greater than reality [185]
	Hepworth (1999) Students not retaining information literacy skills
	Dunnington and Strong (2006) Student confidence levels improved but actual skills did not [635]
	Coupe (1993) Student skill levels did not improve
	Schuck (1992) Instruction course produced no improvements
Observed Behavior	
	Hartmann (2001) Participation in information literacy is driven by professor requirements [focus groups]
	Turnbull et al. (2000) Students reluctant to seek and use information
	Kuh and Gonyea (2003) Library experiences do not lead to gains in information literacy [300,000]

Numbers in square brackets are the sample sizes.

In summarizing the information literacy literature, a fairly clear picture comes into focus:

- A majority of the literature has centered on the testing of discrete skills to improve the delivery of information literacy content. Such a perspective focuses on the instructor, instructor method, and/or instruction materials and is too narrowly focused.

- Little research has addressed the value of improved information literacy skills and success in the academic environment.

- No research has been done to determine the extent to which good information literacy skills assist in lifelong learning and greater success in student careers after graduation—a "big picture" perspective.

Evaluation of Reference Services

The vast majority of "library centric" studies examining the quality of reference services are, by design, internally focused and consider such topics as the reference interval, service times, queuing times, librarian-customer interactions, accuracy of the provided information, and so forth. In general, despite the many reference accuracy studies, there are inconsistent operational definitions of "accuracy" and outcome variables included in the analysis. Other problems with most of these studies include simplistic statistical analysis and a lack of random sampling.[92]

The accuracy of information provided by reference services has the potential for some serious negative consequences, depending on how the information will be used. Paul Burton provided a summary of the numerous studies in this area and suggests that other professionals do not get it wrong 45 percent of the time. Burton recommends that librarians do more research into the contribution of information to work that users do and the environment in which their information needs arise.[93]

More recently, Andrew Hubbertz has raised three fundamental concerns about unobtrusive testing used to assess reference accuracy, citing serious concerns about this type of research.[94] His methodological concerns are

- That all libraries in such tests must be administered the same standardized test—in other words, be asked the same questions. This will allow the identification of varying results to a single variable—library performance. Wondering about the wide variation in accuracy results, Hubbertz states that the difficulty of the questions or the skill, experience, training, and tenacity of the librarian could account for the differences since the same questions were not administered at all locations.

- Such tests are principally useful for measuring relative performance rather than assessing the overall quality of service. Typically, possible questions are pre-tested and those that score higher than 75 percent or lower than 25 percent are rejected. In reality, the range of accuracy scores varies from about 35 to 80 percent—about what one should expect given the design of the tests.[95] Hubbertz re-analyzed the two government depository studies and sorted the questions into "easy" and "hard" categories based on accuracy success. Overall, Charles McClure and Peter Hernon reported a 37 percent accuracy rate—the "easy" questions had a corresponding rate of 52 percent and the "hard" questions a 23 percent rate. Similarly, the Juris Dilevko and Elizabeth Dolan study reported that full depository libraries had an accuracy rate of 37 percent—the "easy" questions had a 46 percent rate and the "hard" questions a 29 percent accuracy rate.[96]

- This type of test should be used for the evaluation of reference collections and assessing the various modes of delivering service—in-person, 24/7 virtual reference, telephone, e-mail, chat, and so forth. Accuracy information about the comparative performance of each mode would be helpful to almost every library.

The value of information provided to the student or faculty member depends on the situation of need and the prior knowledge of the user, among other variables, and what is valuable to one individual may not necessarily be valuable to another. The value of the information or services may be affected by the users' attitudes toward the service and staff. If the users appreciate a service, they are more likely to accord it a high value.

A few studies used a technique developed by market researchers to develop a model of users' preferences for a particular product or service when all the attributes are considered together. This technique, called conjoint analysis, allows all levels of each attribute to be compared to all levels of the other attributes. Applied within the context of academic reference services, several studies found that college students prefer a definite answer (rather than uncertainty) for which they had to wait only a brief period of time, and that the answer was provided in a timely manner.[97]

One survey used the contingent valuation method to estimate the economic value that patrons attach to reference desk service at the Virginia Commonwealth University. David Harless and Frank Allen found that students were willing to pay $5.59 per semester to maintain current hours of the reference, desk while instructional faculty were willing to pay $45.76 per year to maintain current hours.[98]

The Wisconsin-Ohio Reference Evaluation Program (WOREP) asks the library patron to complete a short checklist about his or her query, and the librarian fills out a corresponding checklist. A transaction is scored as successful only when the customer reports finding exactly what was wanted, marks being fully satisfied, and does not check any of the nine listed reasons for dissatisfaction. An analysis of 7,013 reference transactions in 74 general reference departments in academic libraries around the United States found a mean success rate of 57 percent. Further analysis revealed that 46 percent of medium-sized libraries give quality reference service, compared to 30 percent of small libraries and 28 percent of large libraries.[99] Not surprisingly, having insufficient time for most customers and their questions usually had a negative effect on success in all sizes of libraries. The use of WOREP allows a library to discover its strengths and weaknesses and to compare itself to a set of peer libraries that have also completed the WOREP survey.

The quality and costs of providing reference services are becoming much more visible. A recent study at Cornell University indicated that Google Answers, an e-Bay-like marketplace for people with questions and others who are prepared to answer these questions, was significantly less expensive than comparable reference services at Cornell. Cornell was twice as expensive, and the Google Answers responses were nearly as good as the responses of the reference librarians.[100] And 94 percent of the students who used Google Answers indicated that they would use the service again. (**Note:** Google Answers is no longer available.)

Evaluation of the Library

Most academic library surveys address issues of user satisfaction, quality of service, and access. For example, the University of Northern Colorado library conducted a survey that had 694 respondents (out of a spring 1990 enrollment of 7,397—a 9 percent sample). Self-reported "excellent or good" library skills improved from the freshman to senior years. A section of the survey included an objective test of library skills—questions pertaining to the *four* components of information literacy (identifying, finding, evaluating, and using relevant tools, services, information, and materials). An analysis of these test questions revealed no increased proficiency from the freshman to senior years.[101]

In recent years academic libraries have been using user satisfaction surveys to evaluate the library and its services. A satisfaction survey asks the client to assess the quality and utility of library services. A customer satisfaction survey affords the library an opportunity to learn what matters to students and faculty and then apply the results to improve service delivery. It should not be surprising that there can often be different perspectives about the quality of service being provided. One study found that academic librarians underestimate the importance of the responsiveness of a service to their customers while they overestimate the importance of the characteristics of staff that provide the service.[102] In the end, the only assessment of service quality that matters is the customer's; all other judgments are essentially irrelevant.

Customer satisfaction, by its very nature, is inward and backward looking (a lagging indicator of performance). A customer's experience with a library and its services is dictated by a simple formula:

$$\text{Customer satisfaction} = \text{Performance} - \text{Expectations}^{103}$$

The Association of Research Libraries (ARL) developed a service quality survey tool for libraries called LibQUAL+. LibQUAL+ is based on the work of Berry, Parasuraman, and Zeithaml, who developed a service quality assessment tool called SERQUAL for the retail industry. The LibQUAL+ has been evolving over several years, so that by late 2006 more than 700 libraries had used the tool.

LibQUAL+ provides information about three dimensions of library service quality: affect of service, library as place, and information control. The survey has 22 questions that focus on these three dimensions. Eight additional questions ask about information literacy and general satisfaction. This is followed by questions pertaining to library use and demographics and an opportunity for the respondent to provide additional comments in an open-ended field. Interestingly, about 40 percent of the respondents provide open-ended comments. This provides the library with a wealth of information that can be analyzed to identify common themes about problem areas and also about services that are being well received.

The Web-based LibQUAL+ instrument identifies three customer perceptions: minimal, optimal, and current service levels. The area between minimal and optimal expectations is a user-defined zone of tolerance. The differences between these customer perceptions lead to gaps of service, which can be further analyzed using other tools. The value of LibQUAL+ to the individual library is that the perception of quality of service levels can be tracked over time.[104] In addition, the library can prepare an analysis to discover any service gaps and gain a better understanding of its existing customer concerns through the reading and analysis of the open-ended comments.

John V. Lombardi, chancellor and professor of history at the University of Massachusetts Amherst, was the keynote speaker at the Academic Library Assessment Conference held in Charlottesville, Virginia, on September 25, 2006. Lombardi was asked to speak about "library performance measures that matter" and suggested that in the highly competitive environment on a university campus, good LibQUAL+ scores from undergraduates are meaningless since these surveys tell the administration how much people "love you." Such surveys do not tell the chancellor why the library deserves more money than any other department. Clearly universities are a very competitive environment in which each department is competing against the others for scarce resources.

Chancellor Lombardi wanted to know what difference the library makes in the lives of students, teaching faculty, and researchers. Faced with a multi-million-dollar decision to renovate the library in the near future, Lombardi suggested it might be prudent to shift the library materials to an off-site storage facility and convert the existing library into a "study hall." Will libraries become a part of institutional teaching and learning centers, or will these activities become a part of the library? Lombardi is looking for outcome measures, since these are the measures that matter!

Accreditation Library Self-Studies

The seven regional accreditation commissions have clear expectations when it comes to the data that should be presented by a library as a result of its self-study. The commissions are beginning to ask the academic library to demonstrate the impact of the library in the lives of the institution's students and faculty. Rather than relying on input measures, such as size of collections and the library's budget, the commissions are asking for evidence of the quality, accessibility, relevance, availability, and delivery of resources and services, regardless of the location of the library's customers.

The accreditation commissions are asking the library to demonstrate library impacts or outcomes by employing library usage data organized by academic programs, assess the role of the library in curriculum development, and provide an evaluation of what students learn from information literacy programs.

For example, the Western Association of Schools and Colleges asks its member institutions to relate student learning to the use of library resources. Specifically, Standard 2.3 states:

> The institution's expectations for learning and student attainment are clearly reflected in its academic programs and policies. These include . . . the use of its library and information resources.[105]

Among the topics that typically must be addressed by a library's self-study are

- access, availability, and use of library collections;
- collections and learning resources;
- information literacy;
- information technology;
- collaboration with faculty and other academic staff;
- library staff; and
- outcomes assessment.

Historically, libraries have focused the majority of their efforts on collecting and documenting data pertaining to the first six topics. Yet the last topic, outcomes assessment, has recently become a concern of the accreditation commissions, and it is likely to occupy the attention of most academic library directors in the future.

Library as Place

> *Universities today do a great job of providing access to the technologies and materials of scholarship, but they are doing a poor job of providing the conditions, the space and time, that support the contemplative side, the intellectus, of scholarly work.*
>
> —David M. Levy [106]

The physical space in academic libraries has undergone considerable change in the past decade. Not only have the additional technologies necessary to provide students with the tools to use library resources successfully been accommodated, but also space has been provided so students can engage in cooperative learning. Group study spaces are provided along with software tools so students can work together to complete shared assignments. Some have called the library that provides access to integrated technology, group study space, and individual study areas the "Information Commons" or "Learning Commons." The University of Texas library moved 90,000 volumes from its undergraduate library to other campus libraries to create its Information Commons. [107]

Perhaps the most challenging aspect of the Commons initiatives is meeting student demand for 24-hour access. Increased staffing requirements and staff training can be demanding in an effort to keep pace with technology changes, system upgrades, and implementation of new capabilities that library customers assume are a given, such as wireless access.

As yet there have been no objective evaluations of the success and limitations of the Information Commons concept being employed at a number of academic libraries. [108] Yet their popularity and intensive use by students seem to attest to a continuing role for the "library as place."

Two surveys were conducted at the University of Delaware to determine what students were doing in the library (surveys were returned by 23 percent of those approached). The primary reason for attendance in the library was to use it as a place to study. [109]

More recently, the University of Iowa conducted a survey of graduate and professional students and found that although these students come to the library to do research or use other library resources, few come to study or borrow materials. When students do come to the library, they recognize the need for assistance and prefer human contact and instruction. [110]

Another study at the Mississippi State University found that using the library as a place to study and socialize was a significant determinant of the average weekly time students spent in the library. It was found that male students, white students, students with high ACT scores, students with full-time jobs, and students living off campus will spend less time in the library than their counterparts.[111] A survey of undergraduate students at the University of Rhode Island found that while a majority of students believed they were effective seekers and users of library services, 40 percent were not satisfied with their search for information and materials found.[112]

Providing a confounding view, a survey at the University of Southern California found that undergraduates came to the library to study alone (81 percent), use a computer for class work (61 percent), and study with a group (55 percent). Slightly more than one-third (36 percent) came to check out a book, and even fewer came to use print journals (12 percent) or get research assistance (13 percent).[113] Similar results were found in a study by Qun Jiao and Anthony Onwuegbuzie.[114]

Summary

Academic libraries confront two major problems when attempting to describe the impact of their services on desired organizational goals and objectives:

- The libraries are not strategically or externally focused when attempting to select measures to use as evidence of how they affect educational outcomes.

- Library data and performance measures are not organized in ways that are meaningful to campus administrators or accreditation teams. And often the library performance measures cannot be linked to campuswide planning documents, goals and objectives, and outcomes.[115]

The quality of undergraduate education is more about what is done programmatically than the resource base of an institution.[116] Two key predictors of academic success are the duration and quality of student-faculty interactions and the quality of the students' interpersonal life on campus.

Academic libraries need to move their assessment activities from an internal focus to one that articulates and demonstrates evidence of their impact on an undergraduate education. Thus, libraries need to move beyond their traditional focus on resource measures to a way of identifying educational impacts. Two important questions for a library to ask are: How can we influence faculty–student interactions? and How can the library contribute to an improved student interpersonal life?

Notes

1. W. E. Troutt. Regional Accreditation Evaluation Criteria and Quality Assurance. *Journal of Higher Education*, 50 (2), 1979, 199–210.

2. R. Nichols. Effects of Various College Characteristics on Student Aptitude Test Scores. *Journal of Educational Psychology*, 55 (1), 1964, 45–54.

3. A. Astin. Undergraduate Achievement and Institutional "Excellence." *Science*, 161, 1968, 661–68.

4. D. A. Rock, J. A. Centra, and R. L. Linn. Relationship Between College Characteristics and Student Achievement. *American Educational Research Journal*, 7, 1970, 109–21.

5. A. Paul Williams. Conceptualizing Academic Library Use: Results of a Survey of Continuing Education Undergraduates in a Small Canadian Undergraduate University. *Canadian Journal of Higher Education*, 25 (3), 1995, 31–48.

6. Ethelene Whitmire. The Relationship Between Undergraduates' Background Characteristics and College Experiences and Their Academic Library Use. *College & Research Libraries*, 62, November 2001, 528–40.

7. Karen de Jager. Library Use and Academic Achievement. *South African Journal of Library & Information Science*, 65 (1), March 1997, 26–30.

8. Charles B. Harrell. The Use of an Academic Library by University Undergraduates. Ph.D. dissertation, University of North Texas, 1988.

9. Whitmire, Relationship Between Undergraduates' Background Characteristics and College Experiences, 528–40.

10. Jennifer Wells. The Influence of Library Usage on Undergraduate Academic Success. *Australian Academic & Research Libraries,* June 1995, 121–28.

11. James M. Donovan. Do Librarians Deserve Tenure? Casting an Anthropological Eye on Role Definition within the Law School. *Law Library Journal*, 88 (3), 1996, 382–401.

12. Gorham Lane. Assessing the Undergraduates' Use of the University Library. *College & Research Libraries*, 27 (4), 1966, 277–82.

13. Lloyd Kramer and Martha Kramer. The College Library and the Drop-Out. *College & Research Libraries*, 29 (4), 1968, 310–12.

14. Patrick Barkey. Patterns of Student Use of a College Library. *College & Research Libraries*, 26 (3), 1965, 115–18.

15. Jane Hiscock. Does Library Usage Affect Academic Performance? *Australian Academic & Research Libraries*, 17 (4), December 1986, 207–13.

16. Tony Mays. Do Undergraduates Need Their Libraries? *Australian Academic & Research Libraries*, 17 (2), June 1986, 56–62.

17. Rachel Applegate. Faculty Information Assignments: A Longitudinal Examination of Variations in Survey Results. *The Journal of Academic Librarianship*, 32 (4), July 2006, 355–63.

18. Linda K. Rambler. Syllabus Study: Key to a Responsive Academic Library. *Journal of Academic Librarianship*, 8, July 1982, 155–59.

19. George D. Kuh and Robert M Gonyea. The Role of the Academic Library in Promoting Student Engagement in Learning. *College & Research Libraries*, 64, 2003, 256–82.

20. James Self. Reserve Readings and Student Grades: Analysis of a Case Study. *Library & Information Science Research*, 9 (1), January–March 1987, 29–40.

21. Kathy Schulz. Your Place or Mine? Use of Patron-Initiated Interlibrary Loan vs. the Local Library Collection Among Undergraduates at OhioLINK Schools. *Collection Management*, 26 (4), 2001, 15–28.

22. Anna M. Van Scoyco and Caroline Cason. The Electronic Academic Library: Undergraduate Behavior in a Library Without Books. *portal: Libraries and the Academy*, 6 (1), 2006, 47–58.

23. Carol Tenopir. *Use and Users of Electronic Library Resources: An Overview and Analysis of Recent Research Studies.* Washington, DC: Council on Library and Information Resources, 2003. Available online at http://www.clir.org/pubs/reports/pub120/contents.html (accessed March 21, 2007).

24. Steve Hiller. The Impact of Information Technology and Online Library Resources on Research, Teaching and Library Use at the University of Washington. *Performance Measurement & Metrics*, 3 (3), 2002, 134–39.

25. Brinley Franklin and Terry Plum. "Successful Web Survey Methodologies for Measuring the Impact of Networked Electronic Services (MINES for Libraries)." *IFLA Journal* 32 (1), 2006, 28–40; and Brinley Franklin, Martha Kyrillidou, and Toni Olshen. *The Story Behind the Numbers: Measuring the Impact of Networked Electronic*

Services (MINES) and the Assessment of the Ontario Council of University Libraries' Scholars Portal. Presented at the 6th Northumbria International Conference on Performance Measurement in Libraries and Information Services, Durham, England, August 22–23, 2005.

26. Kimberly B. Kelley and Gloria J. Orr. Trends in Distant Student Use of Electronic Resources: A Survey. *College & Research Libraries,* 64 (3), 2003, 176–91.

27. Carol H. Montgomery and Donald W. King. Comparing Library and User Related Cost of Print and Electronic Journal Collections: A First Step Towards a Comprehensive Analysis. *D-Lib Magazine,* 8 (10), October 2002. Available online at http://dlib.org/dlib/october02/ montgomery/10montgomery.html (accessed March 21, 2007).

28. Centre for Research in Lifelong Learning. *Student Evaluation Project. Survey of Progression and Retention 2001/2002: Report Three.* Glasgow, UK: Glasgow Caledonian University, 2003, reported in John Crawford, Angel De Vincente, and Stuart Clink. Use and Awareness of Electronic Information Services by Students at Glasgow Caledonian University: A Longitudinal Study. *Journal of Librarianship & Information Science,* 36 (3), September 2004, 101–17.

29. Vincent Kiernan. Professors Are Unhappy with Limitations of Online Resources, Survey Finds. *The Chronicle of Higher Education,* 50, April 30, 2004, A34.

30. Donald W. King, Sarah Aerni, Fern Brody, Matt Hebison, and Amy Knapp. *The Use and Outcomes of University Library Print and Electronic Collections.* Pittsburgh: University of Pittsburgh, Sara Fine Institute for Interpersonal Behavior and Technology, April 2004; and Donald W. King, Sarah Aerni, Fern Brody, Matt Hebison, and Paul Kohberger. *Comparative Cost of the University of Pittsburgh Electronic and Print Library Collections.* Pittsburgh: University of Pittsburgh, Sara Fine Institute for Interpersonal Behavior and Technology, May 2004. See also Roger C. Schonfeld, Donald W. King, Ann Okerson, and Eileen Gifford Fenton. Library Periodicals Expenses: Comparison of Non-Subscription Costs of Print and Electronic Formats on a Life-Cycle Basis. *D-Lib Magazine,* 10 (1), January 2004. Available at http://www.dlib.org/dlib/january04/ schonfeld/01schonfeld.html (accessed March 21, 2007); and Donald W. King, Carol Tenopir, Carol Hansen Montgomery, and Sarah E. Aerni. Patterns of Journal Use by Faculty at Three Diverse Universities. *D-Lib Magazine,* 9 (10), October 2003. Available at http://www. dlib.org/dlib/october03/king/10king.html (accessed March 21, 2007).

31. Among these are Loyola University, New Orleans. See Darla Rushing and Deborah Poole. The Role of the Library in Student Retention, in Maurice Caitlin Kelly and Andrea Kross, eds., *Making the Grade: Libraries and Student Success*. Chicago: Association for Academic & Research Libraries, 2002.

32. Stanley Wilder. Library Jobs and Student Retention. *College & Research Libraries*, 51 (11), 1990, 1035–38.

33. Tom Eadie. Immodest Proposals: User Instruction for Students Does Not Work. *Library Journal*, 115 (17), October 15, 1990, 44.

34. Commission on Higher Education. *Characteristics of Excellence in Higher Education: Standards for Accreditation*. Philadelphia: Middle States Association Commission on Higher Education, 1990, 35–36.

35. John C. Selegean, Martha Lou Thomas, and Marie Louise Richman. Long-Range Effectiveness of Library Use Instruction. *College & Research Libraries*, 44 (6), November 1983, 476–80.

36. Richard Werking. Evaluating Bibliographic Instruction: A Review and Critique. *Library Trends*, 29, Summer 1980, 153–72.

37. Tom Eadie. Beyond Immodesty: Questioning the Benefits of BI. *RQ*, 21, 1982, 331–33.

38. Eric Landrum and Diana Muench. Assessing Student Library Skills and Knowledge: The Library Research Strategies Questionnaire. *Psychological Reports*, 75, 1994, 1617–24.

39. Cathy Moore-Jansen. What Difference Does It Make? One Study of Student Background and the Evaluation of Library Instruction. *Research Strategies*, 15 (1), 1997, 26–38.

40. Larry Hardesty, Nicholas P. Lovrich Jr., and James Mannon. Library-Use Instruction: Assessment of Long-Term Effects. *College & Research Libraries*, 43 (1), 1982, 38–46.

41. Donna Corlett. Library Skills, Study Habits and Attitudes, and Sex as Related to Academic Achievement. *Educational and Psychological Measurement*, 34 (4), 1974, 967–69.

42. Deborah Moore, Steve Brewster, Cynthia Dorroh, and Michael Moreau. Information Competency Instruction in a Two-Year College: One Size Does Not Fit All. *Reference Services Review*, 30, November 2002, 300–306.

43. Susan A. Ware, J. Deena, and A. Morganti. Competency-Based Approach to Assessing Workbook Effectiveness. *Research Strategies*, 4 (9), 1986, 4–10.

44. Nancy W. Colborn and Rossane M. Cordell. Moving from Subjective to Objective Assessments of Your Instruction Program. *Reference Services Review*, 26, Fall/Winter 1998, 125–37.

45. John S. Riddle and Karen A. Hartman. But Are They Learning Anything? Designing an Assessment of First Year Library Instruction. *College & Undergraduate Libraries*, 7, 2000, 66.

46. Patricia S. Breivik. Brooklyn College: A Test Case, in *Open Admissions and the Academic Library*. Chicago: American Library Association, 1977.

47. Amy Dykeman and Barbara King. Term Paper Analysis: A Proposal for Evaluating Bibliographic Instruction. *Research Strategies*, 1, December 1983, 14–21; David F. Kohl and Lizabeth A. Wilson. Effectiveness of Course Integrated Bibliographic Instruction in Improving Course Work. *RQ*, 26, December 1986, 203–11; and David N. King and John C. Ory. Effects of Library Instruction on Student Research: A Case Study. *College & Research Libraries*, 42 (1), January 1981, 31–41.

48. Mark Emmons and Wanda Martin. Engaging Conversation: Evaluating the Contribution of Library Instruction to the Quality of Student Research. *College & Research Libraries*, 63 (6), November 2002, 545–60.

49. Rui Wang. The Lasting Impact of a Library Credit Course. *portal: Libraries and the Academy*, 6 (1), January 2006, 79–92.

50. Selegean, Thomas, and Richman. Long-Range Effectiveness of Library Use Instruction, 476–80.

51. Hardesty, Lovrich, and Mannon. Library-Use Instruction, 38–46.

52. Donald Barclay. Evaluating Library Instruction: Doing the Best You Can with What You Have. *RQ*, 33, Winter 1993, 194–99.

53. Barclay, Evaluating Library Instruction, 196.

54. Elizabeth Carter. "Doing the Best You Can with What You Have": Lessons Learned from Outcomes Assessment. *The Journal of Academic Librarianship*, 28 (1), January–March 2002, 36–41.

55. Jill Coupe. Undergraduate Library Skills: Two Surveys at Johns Hopkins University. *Research Strategies*, 11 (4), Fall 1993, 187–201.

56. Debbie Malone and Carol Videon. Assessing Undergraduate Use of Electronic Resources: A Quantitative Analysis of Works Cited. *Research Strategies*, 15 (3), 1997, 151–58.

57. David Eyman and Alven Nunley. *Effectiveness of Library Science 101 in Teaching Bibliographic Skills*. ERIC Document ED150 962, May 1977.

58. Stephen K. Stoan. Research and Library Skills: An Analysis and Interpretation. *College & Research Libraries*, 45, March 1984, 103.

59. Sara J. Penhale, Nancy Taylor, and Thomas G. Kirk. *A Method of Measuring the Reach of a Bibliographic Instruction Program*. Available at www.ala.org/ala/acrlbucket/nashville1997pap/penhaletaylor.htm (accessed March 21, 2007).

60. M. Shanley and C. Witten. University 101 Freshman Seminar Course: A Longitudinal Study of Persistence, Retention, and Graduation Rates. *NASPA Journal*, 27, 1990, 344–52.

61. C. Wilkie and S. Kuckuck. A Longitudinal Study of the Effects of a Freshman Seminar. *Journal of the Freshman Year Experience*, 1, 1989, 7–16.

62. K. Ketkar and S. D. Bennett. Strategies for Evaluating a Freshman Studies Program. *Journal of the Freshman Year Experience*, 1, 1989, 33–44.

63. J. Benton. Bibliographic Instruction: A Radical Assessment, in C. Oberman-Soroka, ed., *Proceedings from the Second Southeastern Conference on Approaches to Bibliographic Instruction, 22–23 March 1979*. Charleston, SC: College of Charleston, 1980, 53–68.

64. Ernest T. Pascarella and Patrick T. Terenzini. *How College Affects Students: Findings and Insights From Twenty Years of Research*. San Francisco: Jossey-Bass, 1991, 118.

65. Available at http://harcourtassessment.com (accessed March 21, 2007).

66. Ethelene Whitmire. Academic Library Performance Measures and Undergraduates' Library Use and Educational Outcomes. *Library & Information Science Research*, 24, 2002, 107–28.

67. Ethelene Whitmire. Development of Critical Thinking Skills: An Analysis of Academic Library Experiences and Other Measures. *College & Research Libraries*, 59 (3), May 1998, 1–8.

68. Patrick T. Terenzini and Leonard Springer. Influences Affecting the Development of Students' Critical Thinking Skills. *Research in Higher Education*, 36 (1), 1995, 23–40; and Patrick T. Terenzini and Leonard Springer. First-Generation College Students: Characteristics, Experiences, and Cognitive Development. *Research in Higher Education*, 37 (1), 1996, 1–23.

69. Patricia S. Breivik and Gordon Gee. *Information Literacy: Revolution in the Library*. New Your: American Council on Education/ Macmillan, 1989; and Patricia S. Breivik. *Student Learning in the Information Age*. Phoenix: American Council on Education/Oryx, 1998.

70. Topsy N. Smalley. College Success: High School Librarians Make the Difference. *The Journal of Academic Librarianship*, 30 (3), May 2004, 193–98.

71. Laurie A. MacWhinnie. The Information Commons: The Academic Library of the Future. *portal: Libraries and the Academy*, 3 (2), 2003, 241–57.

72. Available at www.ala.org/ala/acrl/acrlstandards/ informationliteracy competency. htm (accessed March 21, 2007).

73. Andrea L. Foster. Students Fall Short on "Information Literacy," Educational Testing Service's Study Finds. *The Chronicle of Higher Education*, 53 (10), October 27, 2006, A36.

74. Ethelene Whitmire. Factors Influencing Undergraduates' Self-Reported Satisfaction with Their Information Literacy Skills. *portal: Libraries and the Academy*, 1 (4), 2001, 409–20.

75. Heidi Julien and Stuart Boon. Assessing Instructional Outcomes in Canadian Academic Libraries. *Library & Information Science Research*, 26, 2004, 121–39.

76. Chris Brewer. Integrating Information Literacy into the Health Sciences Curriculum: Longitudinal Study of an Information Literacy Program for the University of Wollongong. Paper presented at the 4th National information Literacy Conference, Adelaide, South Australia, December 1999.

77. Julie Rabine and Catherine Cardwell. Start Making Sense: Practical Approaches to Outcomes Assessment for Libraries. *Research Strategies*, 17 (4), 2000, 319–35.

78. Patricia Davitt Maughan. Assessing Information Literacy among Undergraduates: A Discussion of the Literature and the University of California-Berkeley Assessment Experience. *College & Research Libraries*, 62 (1), January 2001, 71–85.

79. Mark Hepworth. A Study of Undergraduate Information Literacy and Skills: The Inclusion of Information Literacy and Skills in the Undergraduate Curriculum. Paper presented at the 65th IFLA Council and General Conference, Bangkok, Thailand, August 20–28, 1999. Available at http://www.ifla.org/IV/ifla65/papers/107-124e.htm (accessed March 21, 2007).

80. Joan R. Kaplowitz and Janice Contini. Computer Assisted Instruction: Is It an Option for Bibliographic Instruction in Large Undergraduate Survey Classes? *College & Research Libraries*, 59 (1), 1998, 19–27.

81. Angela Dunnington and Mary Lou Strong. What's Assessment Got to Do with It?! Exploring Student Learning Outcomes. Presentation given at the ALA Annual Conference, New Orleans, Louisiana June 24, 2006. Personal communication with the author.

82. Jill Coupe. Undergraduate Library Skills: Two Surveys at John Hopkins University. *Research Strategies*, 11, Fall 1993, 188–201.

83. Brian R. Schuck. Assessing a Library Instruction Program. *Research Strategies*, 10, Fall 1992, 152–60.

84. See the Project SAILS Web site at www.projectsails.org.

85. Elizabeth Hartmann. Understandings of Information Literacy: The Perceptions of First-Year Undergraduate Students at the University of Ballarat. *Australian Academic & Research Libraries*, 32 (2), 2001, 110–22.

86. Deborah Turnbull, Denise Frost, and Nicola Foxlee. Infoseek, InfoFind! Information Literacy and Integrated Service Delivery for Researchers and Postgraduates. Paper presented at the Information Online 2003 Conference, Sydney, New South Wales, January 2003; and Margaret C. Wallace, Allison Shorten, and Patrick Crookes. Teaching Information Literacy Skills: An Evaluation. *Nurse Education Today*, 20, 2000, 485–89.

87. Jillian R. Griffiths and Peter Brophy. Student Searching Behavior and the Web: Use of Academic Resources and Google. *Library Trends*, 53 (4), Spring 2005, 539–54.

88. Steve Jones. The Internet Goes to College: How Students are Living in the Future with Today's Technology. *Pew Internet and American Life Project*. Available at http://www.pewinternet.org/pdfs/PIP_College_Report.pdf (accessed March 21, 2007).

89. Cathy De Rosa, Joanne Cantrell, Janet Hawk, and Alane Wilson. *College Students' Perceptions of Libraries and Information Resources*. Dublin, OH: OCLC, 2006.

90. George D. Kuh and Robert M. Gonyea. The Role of the Academic Library in Promoting Student Engagement in Learning. *College & Research Libraries*, 64 (7), July 2003, 256–82.

91. James W. Marcum. Rethinking Information Literacy. *The Library Quarterly*, 72 (1), January 2002, 1–26.

92. Matthew L. Saxton. Reference Service Evaluation and Meta-Analysis: Findings and Methodological Issues. *Library Quarterly*, 67 (3), July 1997, 267–89.

93. Paul F. Burton. Accuracy of Information Provision: The Need for Client-Centered Service. *Journal of Librarianship*, 22 (4), October 1990, 210–15.

94. Andrew Hubbertz. The Design and Interpretation of Unobtrusive Evaluations. *Reference & User Services Quarterly*, 44 (4), Summer 2005, 327–35.

95. Terence Crowley. Half-Right Reference: Is It True? *RQ*, 25 (1), Fall 1985, 59–68.

96. Juris Dilevko and Elizabeth Dolan. Government Documents Reference Service in Canada: A Nationwide Unobtrusive Study of Public and Academic Depository Libraries. *Library & Information Science Research*, 22 (2), 2000, 185–222.

97. Gregory A. Crawford. A Conjoint Analysis of Reference Services in Academic Libraries. *College & Research Libraries*, 55, May 1994, 257–67; Michael Halperin and Maureen Stardon. Measuring Students' Preferences for Reference Service: A Conjoint Analysis. *Library Quarterly*, 50, 1980, 208–24; and Kenneth D. Ramsing and John R. Wish. What Do Library Users Want? A Conjoint Measurement Technique May Yield the Answer. *Information Processing and Management*, 18, 1982, 237–42.

98. David W. Harless and Frank R. Allen. Using the Contingent Valuation Method to Measure Patron Benefits of Reference Desk Service in an Academic Library. *College & Research Libraries*, 60 (1), January 1999, 56–69.

99. John C. Stalker and Marjorie E. Murfin. Quality Reference Service: A Preliminary Case Study. *The Journal of Academic Librarianship*, 22 (6), November 1996, 423–29.

100. Anne R. Kennedy, Nancy Y. McGovern, Ida T. Martinez, and Lance J. Heidig. Google Meet eBay: What Academic Librarians Can Learn from Alternative Information Providers. *D-Lib Magazine*, 9 (6), June 2003. Available at http://www.dlib.org/dlib/june03/kenney/ 06kenney. html (accessed March 21, 2007).

101. Arlene Greer, Lee Weston, and Mary Alm. Assessment of Learning Outcomes: A Measure of Progress in Library Literacy. *College & Research Libraries*, 52 (11), November 1991, 549–57.

102. Susan Edwards and Mairead Browne. Quality in Information Services: Do Users and Librarians Differ in Their Expectations? *Library & Information Science Research*, 17 (2), 1995, 163–85.

103. Richard L. Lynch and Kevin F. Cross. *Measure Up! Yardsticks for Continuous Improvement*. London: Basil Blackwell, 1991.

104. More information about LibQUAL+ may be obtained by visiting their Web site at http://www.libqual.org/.

105. The Western Association of Schools and Colleges. Standard 2. Achieving Educational Objectives Through Core Functions. Teaching and Learning. Criteria for Review, 2.3, in *Handbook of Accreditation*, 2001. Available at http://www.wascsenior.org/wasc/Doc_Lib/2001%20Handbook.pdf (accessed March 21, 2007).

106. David M. Levy. Contemplating Scholarship in the Digital Age. *RBM: A Journal of Rare Books, Manuscripts, and Cultural Heritage*, 6 (2), Fall 2005, 74–75.

107. Katherine S. Mangan. Packing up the Books. *The Chronicle of Higher Education*, 51 (43), July 1 2005.

108. Laurie A. MacWhinnie. The Information Commons: The Academic Library of the Future. *portal: Libraries and the Academy*, 3 (2), 2003, 241–57.

109. Gorham Lane. Assessing the Undergraduates' Use of the University Library. *College & Research Libraries*, 27 (4), 1966, 277–82.

110. Hope Barton. Identifying the Resources and Service Needs of Graduate and Professional Students. *portal: Libraries and the Academy*, 2 (1), January 2002, 125–43.

111. Paul W. Grimes and Marybeth F. Charters. Library Use and the Undergraduate Economics Student. *College Student Journal*, 34 (4), December 2000, 557–71.

112. Cheryl Ann McCarthy. Students' Perceived Effectiveness Using the University Library. *College & Research Libraries*, 56 (3), May 1995, 221–34.

113. Susan Gardner and Susanna Eng. What Students Want: Generation Y and the Changing Function of the Academic Library. *portal: Libraries and the Academy*, 5 (3), 2005, 405–20.

114. Qun G. Jiao and Anthony J. Onwuegbuzie. Prevalence and Reasons for University Library Usage. *Library Review*, 46 (6), 1997, 411–20.

115. Bonnie Gratch Lindauer. Defining and Measuring the Library's Impact on Campuswide Outcomes. *College & Research Libraries*, 59 (6), November 1998, 546–70.

116. Ernest Pascarella and Patrick Terenzini. Designing Colleges for Greater Learning. *Planning for Higher Education*, 20, Spring 1992, 1–16.

Chapter 6

Institutional Assessment of the Research Environment

Attempting to assess the quality and productivity of the faculty and other researchers on a campus is difficult and problematic. Despite the difficulties, there is clear evidence for faculty, especially at a research university, to be concerned about their research and publication productivity. The often heard refrain "publish or perish," whispered in hallways, more than likely rises to a roar when a faculty member is faced with a promotion decision. Faculty in an academic institution are part of a complex research dynamic that is integral to an academic reward system and the availability of funding, in particular funds from federal government agencies, to support research. This dynamic is complemented by a publishing industry with an expanding need for the communication of research results.

Herb White has observed:

> The purpose of publication is, after all, a twofold one. The first and the most immediately recognized purpose is the communication of findings, sometimes to an eager audience and sometimes to a disinterested one. The former is preferable, but even the latter is acceptable, because the other purpose of scholarly publication is the achievement of academic credit. Unfortunately . . . credit depends less on the quality and more on the quantity of activity in today's academic marketplace.[1]

While the unit of analysis for research productivity can be at the individual, departmental, or institutional level, most of the productivity studies of faculty research performance have focused on individual faculty members.

Academic institutions spend a considerable amount each year on research and development. In 2004, National Science Foundation data revealed that academic institutions spent $42 billion on R&D, with the federal government providing 62 percent of funds, the institutions themselves providing 19 percent of funds, industry contributing some 5 percent, and 14 percent coming from other

97

sources.[2] All federal R&D grants to universities and colleges generated some 710,000 jobs, according to data from the Association of American Universities.[3]

Scholarly Peer Assessments

The first academic quality rankings used scholarly peer assessment as their foundation.[4] Since that time several hundred ratings using scholarly peer assessment as the criterion of quality have been published, most limited to a single academic discipline or professional field. The most frequent ratings seem to be in the social sciences (sociology, psychology, and economics) and two professional fields: engineering and business. Among the better known annual ratings are those published by *U.S. News & World Report*.

> *The annual release of U.S. News & World Report's college rankings brings cries of elation, howls of anger, or muted mutterings in the offices of college administrators throughout the land.*
> —A. P. Sanoff[5]

Several multidisciplinary peer rankings have been developed using such criteria as the quality of the graduate program, the effectiveness of a doctoral program, or the effectiveness in educating research scholars and scientists. Peer rankings are also known as reputational studies.

Two of the better-known reputational studies are Allan Cartter's *An Assessment of Quality in Graduate Education*[6] and its replication, produced by Kenneth Roose and Charles Andersen, *A Rating of Graduate Education*.[7] The Conference Board assessed the quality of doctoral programs in more than 200 doctorate-granting universities in the fields of humanities, social and behavioral sciences, biological sciences, mathematical and physical sciences, and engineering.[8]

Not surprisingly, the development and use of peer rankings have been criticized for a number of reasons:

- They can be a mere compendium of gossip.
- The weights assigned to performance indicators are subjective.
- They correlate highly with department faculty size and publication productivity.
- They are subject to "halo effects"—the prestige of the whole institution rubs off on the department.
- The are invalid due to the "alumni effect"—raters give higher scores to the university from which they graduated.

- It is difficult to define a concept such as "academic quality."

- The peer raters are uninformed about the departments they are asked to rate.

- The "wing" of an academic discipline the peer rater identifies with has an impact.

- Less popular programs in less well-known institutions are often ignored.

- Criteria for measurement are ill-defined.

- The publication rate for a department may be "inflated" by faculty outside the department but within the university.

- Should universities offering doctorates in a few disciplines be grouped with those universities that offer a much larger range of doctoral degrees?[9]

It is safe to say that, despite these criticisms and many more, peer rankings of academic programs and departments are usually measuring publication productivity and faculty members' scholarly prestige.

Individual Attributes of the Researcher

A recent survey of faculty found that they spend slightly more than one-half of their time teaching, another 30 percent doing research, and the remainder performing administrative tasks and public service activities.[10] Faculty at research universities spend more time than average on research, while faculty at liberal arts and two-year institutions spend more time teaching than average. The idea of a teacher-scholar is a myth of higher education. Kenneth Feldman reviewed a large number of studies and found little relationship between student ratings of teaching excellence and various forms of research productivity.[11]

A number of productivity studies have examined a wide range of factors (age, gender, educational background, etc.) that might affect faculty research productivity. While there appears to be a strong age- and experience-productivity relationship (as age and experience increase, productivity also increases up to a point and then levels off), this relationship is mixed in higher education and varies by field.[12] However, it can also be observed that full and more senior professors (particularly in research universities) tend to have more accumulative advantages over most assistant and associate professors, which result in higher levels of productivity.[13]

The departmental or institutional culture also has a strong influence in determining the research performance of individual faculty. Culture relates to the shared values and attitudes in an academic unit or institution. A research-oriented culture exists when faculty and administrators are encouraged to be strong researchers during their graduate training, maintain continuous internal and external communication with other researchers, and hire new faculty with strong research credentials.[14]

Most institutions of higher education allocate little attention to assessing institutional-level research output, given the considerable resources that are devoted to its production. Full-time faculty on average published nearly two refereed or juried publications per year for 1997 and 1998, with the vast majority of this activity being concentrated in research- and doctoral-level institutions.[15] Lionel Lewis found a consistent relationship between the reputational type of rankings developed by Cartter and objective measures of research productivity.[16]

Departmental and Institutional Attributes

One widely studied factor is the impact of organizational and faculty size on enhanced research productivity. Larger departmental size may positively affect research productivity because of

- better collaboration within the research groups (In larger departments, several faculty members may have similar research interests and thus collaborate on joint research projects.);

- the ability to attract higher-quality researchers; and

- greater resources, with more discretion about how the funds are spent.[17]

Other institutional factors affecting research productivity include overhead rates, sponsored research policies, and so forth.

Yet disadvantages obviously exist since the research on faculty size is mixed. Kyvik reported no significant relationship between size and research productivity in Norway, except in the natural sciences. Similar results were reported in a study conducted in the United Kingdom. Contrary results were noted in a study analyzing results in the United States, which found that departmental research productivity was closely related to departmental size (number of faculty members).[18]

It is fairly typical for faculty to rank departments within their field on the basis of total publications.[19] Others have used the number of citations received by an individual faculty member to measure research productivity. Another possible measure is the awards and fellowships received by faculty within a department.

Using a per capita method of measuring the various research outputs of institutions allows for controlling for size, which permits comparisons that illuminate the important differences and similarities among a group of peer institutions.

Research examining productivity and institutional control (public versus private) has also reported mixed results. Jordan and his colleagues found strong support that private institutions were associated with greater academic research productivity.[20] However, another study noted that the effect of institutional control declines after controlling for both research support and the department's reputational rating.[21] Muddying the waters even further, Halil Dunbar and Darrell Lewis found that research productivity in public institutions tends to be noticeably less than in private institutions, controlling for faculty size and other variables.[22]

Other variables have been found to be correlated with research productivity. Among these are annual research spending of the department, the number of students in the department, the percent of faculty with research grants, the quality of the computing resources, monies for travel, and the availability of secretarial assistance and teaching assistants.[23]

Some studies have used student characteristics to assess quality. Among the approaches that have been taken are the proportion of alumni who earned doctoral degrees,[24] number of graduates who had contributed articles to *Scientific American*,[25] number of graduates who gained admission to medical school,[26] average academic ability of entering freshmen,[27] and successful careers of alumni as noted in the biographical data in *Who's Who in Engineering*.[28]

Despite the problem of establishing research output data at the institutional level and measurement problems across institutions, several studies indicated that faculty publication patterns may vary across institutions. One study noted that "accumulative advantage" and "resources and recognition" contribute to research support which, in turn, leads to greater research productivity.[29]

It is interesting to note that almost all of the studies examining the factors that influence research productivity use a single measure of productivity: number of publications. The publications are usually broken down into several categories: refereed journal or not, type of publication, conference presentations, and so forth. Such reliance on a single measure, despite its attractiveness as indicated by an almost universal reliance on the measure, suggests that the results of these studies may have a bias. In some cases a summative index may be constructed from counts of journal publications, conference papers, chapters in books, and books.

Most academic institutions have a research support office (an Office of Institutional Research or whatever it may be called on your campus). This office will track the number of research grant proposals that have been submitted, the number of grants funded, and the amount of funding. Often this information is tracked at the department and/or school level and monitored over time. In addition, the amount of funding received from various sources, such as, federal government agencies, foundations, corporations, and other organizations, will usually be monitored.

Ethelene Whitmire has suggested a model for better understanding faculty research productivity (see Figure 6.1, p. 102).

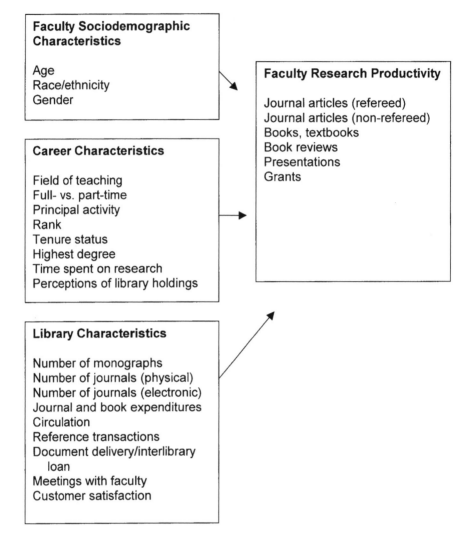

Figure 6.1. Faculty Research Productivity Model. Adapted from Ethelene Whitmire. What Do Faculty Need? Academic Library Resources and Services That Increase Research Productivity, in Hugh A. Thompson, ed., *Proceedings of the ACRL Eleventh National Conference, April 10–13, 2003, Charlotte, North Carolina.*

Institutional Level Assessment

It is interesting to note that the extent to which resources can be used as indicators of quality has not been well understood. While it is often assumed that financial resources are important in nurturing quality, little research evidence exists proving a direct link between the two. In one study, variables such as faculty research productivity and the number and type of degrees awarded were much more important than the availability of financial resources.[30]

Henry Zheng and Alice Stewart prepared an analysis of the 56 public Research I universities as defined by the Carnegie Classification System. Using the data envelopment analysis technique, they compared the research orientation to the instructional orientation for each university using the variables shown in Table 6.1. Using these data they constructed a research performance index and an instructional performance index in order to compare and contrast each university, as shown in Table 6.2.[31] It is interesting to note the dispersion of the universities depending on the teaching or research orientation.

Table 6.1 Attributes Associated with Research Productivity

Individual Attributes	Innate abilities: intelligence, personality, gender, age
	Personal environmental influences: quality of graduate training, culture of employing department
Institutional and Departmental Attributes	Institutional structure and leadership
	• Size of program and number of faculty
	• Type of institution: public or private
	• Amount of university revenue
	• Availability of technology and computing facilities
	Departmental culture and working conditions
	• Workload policies
	• Availability of leave, travel support, and institutional funds for research
	• Number of students on research support
	• "Star" faculty within the department
	• Availability of nongovernmental funds

Table 6.2 Strategic Choices of Universities*

Research Efficiency

Instructional Efficiency	High	Parity	Low
High	Powerhouse Universities N = 7, 13% of sample	Balanced Teaching N = 12, 22% of sample	Teaching Juggernaut N = 16, 29% of sample
Parity	Balanced Research N = 5, 9% of sample	Stuck in Parity N=4, 7% of sample	Treading Water—Teaching N = 3, 5% of sample
Low	Research Juggernaut N = 5, 9% of sample	Treading Water—Research N = 4, 7% of sample	No Focus N = 0

*Adapted from Henry Y. Zheng and Alice C. Stewart. Assessing the Performance of Public Research Universities Using NSF/NCES Data and Data Envelopment Analysis Technique. *AIR Professional File*, 83, Spring 2002.

Charles Oppenheim and David Stuart examined the possible correlation between the investment in an academic library and a higher education's rating in the U.K.'s Research Assessment Exercise (RAE), which involves a peer review of the quality of research produced by each institution. The authors did not find a strong correlation but noted that good universities have both high RAE ratings and good libraries and poor universities have low RAE ratings and less money to spend on libraries.[32]

In a thorough review of prior research, Kenneth Feldman found a weak positive correlation between research productivity and student assessment of teaching effectiveness. Feldman found that the positive association holds when research productivity is measured by publication counts, indicators of research support, and ratings by peers but not when measured by citation counts.[33]

Hugh Graham and Nancy Diamond prepared a historical review and analysis of American research universities using per capita figures to compare institutional output. The authors found that

- the leading private universities have consistently outperformed the best public universities in per capita research productivity, due in part to the greater bureaucratic freedom and fewer regulatory constraints on private universities;

- medical schools and the academic health science centers that surround them benefited greatly by the rapid rise in the National Institute of Health's spending for research; and

- political and business leaders developed state-level versions of industrial policy for higher education to involve universities in regional economic development.[34]

Most universities will track the number and amount of grants received from outside sources, the number of patents, the amount of patent royalties, and the number of jobs generated from research and development activities on campus.

Academic Analytics, a commercial company, has developed a Faculty Scholarly Productivity Index. Faculty members are judged using three factors: publications, which include the number of books and journal articles published; federal grant dollars awarded; and honors and awards. The individual faculty member's score is aggregated into a departmental and university score. The scholarly productivity is expressed as a z-score, a statistical measure that reveals how far and in what direction a value is from the mean. The z-score allows the performance of programs to be compared across disciplines.[35]

Summary

A summary of all the individual and organizational attributes pertaining to research productivity is presented in Table 6.1 (p. 103).

Notes

1. Herbert White. Scholarly Publication, Academic Libraries, and the Assumption That These Processes Are Really Under Management Control. *College & Research Libraries*, 54, July 1993, 295.

2. Available at www.nsf.gov/statistics/seind06/c5/c5h.htm (accessed March 22, 2007).

3. Available at www.aau.edu/resuniv/FY01/Employ.html (accessed March 22, 2007).

4. J. M. Catell. A Further Statistical Study of American Men of Science. *Science*, 32, 1910, 672–88.

5. Alvin P. Sanoff. Rankings Are Here to Stay: Colleges Can Improve Them. *The Chronicle of Higher Education*, 45 (2), September 4, 1999, A96.

6. Allan M. Cartter. *An Assessment of Quality in Graduate Education.* Washington, DC: The American Council on Education, 1966.

7. Kenneth D. Roose and Charles J. Andersen. *A Rating of Graduate Education.* Washington, DC: The American Council on Education, 1970.

8. Lyle V. Jones, Lindzey Gardner, and Porter E. Coggeshall. *An Assessment of Research-Doctorate Programs in the United States.* Washington, DC: The National Academy Press, 1982.

9. David S. Webster. Institutional Effectiveness Using Scholarly Peer Assessments as Major Criteria. *The Review of Higher Education*, 9 (1), 1985, 67–82. See also a wonderful review of such criticisms by W. P. Dolan. *The Ranking Game: The Power of the Academic Elite.* Lincoln: University of Nebraska Press, 1976.

10. Michael F. Middaugh. *Understanding Faculty Productivity: Standards and Benchmarks for Colleges and Universities.* San Francisco: Jossey-Bass, 2001.

11. Kenneth A. Feldman. Research Productivity and Scholarly Accomplishment of College Teachers as Related to Their Instructional Effectiveness: A Review and Exploration. *Research in Higher Education*, 26, 1987, 227–98.

12. Shirley M. Clark and Darrell R. Lewis, eds., *Faculty Vitality and Institutional Productivity: Critical Perspectives for Higher Education.* New York: Teachers College Press, 1985; S. G. Levin and P. E. Stephen. Age and Research Productivity of Academic Scientists. *Research in Higher Education*, 30 (5), 1989, 531–49.

13. J. R. Cole and S. Cole. The Ortega Hypothesis. *Science*, 178, October 27 1972, 368–75; J. S. Long. Productivity and Academic Positions in the Scientific Career. *American Sociological Review*, 43, December 1978, 889–908; Clark and Lewis, *Faculty Vitality and Institutional Productivity.*

14. J. W. Creswell. *Measuring Faculty Research Performance: New Directions for Institutional Research.* San Francisco: Jossey-Bass, 1986.

15. L. J. Zimbler. *Background Characteristics, Work Activities, and Compensation of Faculty and Instructional Staff in Postsecondary Institutions: Fall 1998.* NCES 2001-152. Washington, DC: U.S. Department of Education, 2001, Table 28.

16. Lionel S. Lewis. On Subjective and Objective Rankings of Sociology Departments. *American Sociologist*, 3, May 1968, 129–31.

17. S. Kyvik. Are Big Departments Better Than Small Ones? *Higher Education*, 30 (3), 1995, 295–304.

18. J. M. Jordan, M. Meador, and S. J. Walters. Effects of Departmental Size and Organization on the Research Productivity of Academic Economists. *Economics of Education Review*, 7 (2), 1988, 251–55; J. M. Jordan, M. Meador, and S. J. Walters. Academic Research Productivity, Department Size, and Organization: Further Results. *Economics of Education Review*, 8 (24), 1989, 345–52.

19. K. Borokhovich, R. Bricker, K. Brunarski, and B. Simkins. Finance Research Productivity and Influence. *Journal of Finance*, 50, 1995, 1691–1717; and P. Graves, J. Marchand, and R. Thompson. Economics Departmental Rankings: Research Incentives, Constraints and Efficiency. *American Economic Review*, 72, 1982, 1131–41.

20. Jordan et al., Effects of Departmental Size and Organization on the Research Productivity of Academic Economists.

21. J. Golden and F. V. Carstensen. Academic Research Productivity, Department Size and Organization: Further Results, Rejoinder. *Economics of Education Review*, 11 (2), 1992, 169–71.

22. Halil Dundar and Darrell R. Lewis. Determinants of Research Productivity in Higher Education. *Research in Higher Education*, 39 (6), 1998, 607–31.

23. S. D. Grunig. Research, Reputation, and Resources: The Effect of Research Activity on Perceptions of Undergraduate Education and Institutional Resource Acquisition. *Journal of Higher Education*, 68 (1), 1997, 17–52.

24. R. H. Knapp and J. J. Greenbaum. *The Younger American Scholar: His Collegiate Origins*. Chicago: University of Chicago Press, 1953.

25. Ervin D. Krause and Loretta Krause. The Colleges That Produce Our Best Scientists: A Study of Academic Training Grounds of a Large Group of Distinguished American Scientists. *Science Education*, 54, 1970, 133–40.

26. W. F. Dube. Undergraduate Origins of U.S. Medical Students. *Journal of Medical Education*, 49, 1974, 1005–10.

27. Alexander W. Astin and Lewis C. Solomon. Measuring Academic Quality: An Interim Report. *Change*, 11, 1979, 48–51.

28. Donald D. Glower. A Rational Method for Ranking Engineering Programs. *Engineering Education*, 70, 1980, 788–94, 842.

29. R. Bentley and R. Blackburn. Changes in Academic Research Performance Over Time: A Study of Institutional Accumulative Advantage. *Research in Higher Education*, 31 (4), 1990, 327–45.

30. Walter F. Abbott and Henry M. Barlow. Stratification Theory and Organizational Rank: Resources, Functions and University Prestige in the United States. *Pacific Sociological Review*, 15, October 1972, 401–24.

31. Henry Y. Zheng and Alice C. Stewart. Assessing the Performance of Public Research Universities Using NSF/NCES Data and Data Envelopment Analysis Technique. *AIR Professional File*, 83, Spring 2002.

32. Charles Oppenheim and David Stuart. Is There a Correlation Between Investment in an Academic Library and a Higher Education Institution's Ratings in the Research Assessment Exercise? *Aslib Proceedings*, 56 (3), 2004, 156–65.

33. Kenneth A. Feldman. Research Productivity and Scholarly Accomplishment of College Teachers as Related to Their Instructional Effectiveness: A Review and Exploration. *Research in Higher Education*, 26 (3), 1987, 227–98.

34. Hugh Davis Graham and Nancy Diamond. *The Rise of American Research Universities: Elites and Challengers in the Postwar Era*. Baltimore: Johns Hopkins University Press, 1997.

35. More information about the 2004 and 2005 Faculty Scholarly Productivity Index is available at http://www.academicanalytics.com/ (accessed March 22, 2007).

Chapter

Assessment of the Library's Impact on the Research Environment

Academic libraries are faced with pressure to supply the raw material to be used in the research process. Libraries do this by providing direct access to physical and electronic collections of information resources as well as indirect access to other materials located in other libraries (using interlibrary loan) or from commercial information providers (document delivery). Unfortunately, it is difficult to establish a link to the availability of information resources and research productivity since so many factors come into play. Yet libraries must do a better job of articulating the value of the library and its resources to research productivity.

So how do libraries assist the faculty, researchers, and graduate students in their research efforts? One study examined the number of publication citations across 169 universities in Canada, the United Kingdom, and the United States. A strong relationship existed between the number of institutional associated publications and the number of academic staff, the number of research students, the number of library books and journals, and the level of university revenues.[1] However, the value of these findings, especially those of library holdings, no longer holds given the evidence of other studies.

For example, bigness seems to count at a basic level—large universities produce a large number of publications, and their libraries spend large amounts of money on these and other materials and thus have large collections. Examining the citations in the Institute for Scientific Information (ISI) and library measures derived from the Association of Research Libraries, John Budd found medium to high correlations between the number of publications and number of volumes, materials expenditures, total expenditures, and the number of professional staff.[2] Similar results were noted by James Baughman and Martha Kieltyka.[3]

One study examined the productivity of research and development (R&D) organizations and analyzed the behavior of research managers as perceived by research staff. The managers in the more productive organizations (as defined by rates of growth and return on assets) were characterized by three behaviors:

- They routed literature and references to scientific and technical staff.

- They directed their staff to use more scientific and technical information (STI) and to purchase STI services.

- They encouraged publication of results and supported professional visits and continuing education.[4]

In sum, information-related behavior by managers tended to discriminate between "high-performance" and "low-performance" companies, while non-information-related behavior (planning, making personnel changes, and so forth) did not.

After reviewing a large body of research pertaining to R&D innovation, Joel Goldhar et al. concluded that six characteristics are conducive to technological innovations:

1. Easy access to information by individuals;

2. Free flow of information both into and out of the organization;

3. Rewards for sharing, seeking, and using "new" externally developed information sources;

4. Encouragement of mobility and interpersonal contacts;

5. Rewards for taking risks; and

6. Accepting and adapting to change.[5]

Note that the first three factors involve access to information that can be provided by the library, including desktop access.

Michael Koenig has studied the relationship between research productivity and the information environment using the pharmaceutical industry as the setting. He found that the more productive companies had information environments that were characterized by

- greater openness to outside information,

- somewhat less concern with protecting proprietary information,

- greater use of information systems by the scientists and more encouragement of browsing and serendipity,

- greater technical and subject sophistication of the information services staff (library staff), and

- relative unobtrusiveness of managerial structure and status indicators in the R&D environment.[6]

Many others, most notably Rosabeth Kanter,[7] James Utterback,[8] and Mariam Ginman,[9] have noted that the formal and informal flows of information should freely move up, down, and across the organization. Gerstberger and Allen found a direct relationship between perceived accessibility of information and several measures of utilization. The researchers appeared to follow Zipf's Law of Least Effort: Individuals choose the option to obtain information that involves the least effort.[10] One of the implications of the Gerstberger and Allen study is that improving the quality and/or quantity of library resources will be wasted unless ways are found to bring information to the researchers easily. Victor Rosenberg studied a group of researchers and found that the primary attribute of any information gathering method is its ease of use.[11]

A survey of those involved in R&D work indicated a need for resources that provide access to the work of other professionals in their fields. The researchers noted that their institutions had increased the pressure for faster innovations and for them to contribute to their company's growth. Ninety-one percent of the respondents indicated that access to information generated productivity in excess of their cost and helped to prevent mistakes.[12]

Determining the value of the library's contribution to an institution's research environment will require considerable effort, but determining and communicating this value is becoming increasingly important for the academic library.

As Brinley Franklin has pointed out, educational institutions can prepare a cost analysis study that results in the distribution of the costs libraries incur to support an institution's major functions—including research. A review of a number of institutions that have prepared such a cost analysis found considerable variation in sponsored research usage of the library. Library usage was generally comparable for library materials used in the library, materials checked out, and use of library services. According to Franklin, electronic services that used supporting sponsored research generally mirrored the same levels of usage of library materials and services.[13]

Sarah Pritchard and Bonnie Lindauer have suggested that the assessment of academic libraries should be linked to institutional goals and objectives. And faculty research productivity should be one of the measures to which academic libraries contribute. They both suggested using multiple indicators of faculty research productivity—number and value of grants secured, number of publications, presentations, research reports, creative works, patent applications, and so forth.[14] However, unless the library can establish a clear link between the use of its physical and electronic resources and the output of researchers, such an approach is only an indirect measure of the value of the library.

Using data from the 1993 National Study of Postsecondary Faculty, Fairweather examined a variety of factors that were potentially related to faculty research productivity. He found a positive relationship between the perceived adequacy of university library facilities and faculty research productivity.[15]

Dunbar and Lewis tested a more comprehensive model of faculty research productivity including individual, departmental, and institutional variables, using data from the National Research Council. They found that library expenditures (not necessarily use) were associated with increased research productivity for faculty in the biological sciences, mathematics, and physical sciences.[16] This positive effect may also suggest that institutions that have larger library expenditures and collections also provide more or better resources in other infrastructure.

Most academic libraries have made little or no distinction in differentiating services to support teaching faculty from research-related activities. Most researchers prefer access to a wide range of recent articles rather than to long runs of back issues of print journals.

One recent project used a Web-based survey that measured both in-library and remote usage of networked electronic resources. The project, called MINES for Libraries—Measuring the Impact of Networked Electronic Services—asked survey respondents to indicate the purpose of their searching.[17] The possible categories for using online resources included sponsored (funded) research, instruction/education/departmental research, patient care, and all other activities. The survey discovered that remote users of electronic resources exceed in-library use by a four to one or larger margin. Not surprisingly, those conducting sponsored research use the electronic resources from their offices rather than visiting the library. In addition, in-library and on-campus use of the electronic resources greatly exceeded off-campus usage. Most of the usage for sponsored research was done by faculty, staff, and researchers.[18] Further complicating the issue of gathering information about use of electronic resources is the fact that many faculty and researchers use graduate assistants to do the actual searching for a project.

Grant-funded research accounted for almost one-third of networked electronic services activity, and this searching was done on campus but not from within the library.[19] Brinley Franklin also noted a high correlation between total research and development funding at an educational institution and total library expenditures at research universities.[20] In addition, use of electronic services supporting sponsored research reflected the same amount of use of physical materials and library services.

A survey found that larger and better financed institutions' faculty members tend to perceive greater dependence on their library than their counterparts in small and medium-sized colleges and universities.[21]

Assessment Methods

A number of research activity indexes can be created in addition to tracking the institution's track record of attracting research revenues.

A *journal publication index* is created by counting the number of refereed articles published per faculty member per year. In some cases, a variation of this index assigns more weight to "quality journals"—however "quality" is defined. Another variation is to track the publication patterns of the professors and researchers who are directly involved with a research project. In some cases, this "researcher publication rate" is contrasted with the other faculty members who are not directly involved with research projects. Typically such indexes are created using the Citation Index from the Institute for Scientific Information. It is also possible to identify the most frequently cited authors.

Some time ago, the Institute for Scientific Information introduced the Impact Factor, which is the number of citations generated by a journal (usually over a multiyear period) divided by the number of papers the journal published in that time or, if you will, the average number of cites per paper. Now journals advertise their "goodness" using their impact factor or fail to mention their impact factor if they are not rated highly.

A *research grant income index* is fashioned by tracking the amount of income associated with research grants and projects per faculty member per year. Over time, it is possible to track the growth of research grant income to the university. Most colleges and universities have an Office of Institutional Research that will track this information.

A *master's thesis publication index* is created by calculating the average number of papers published in refereed journals per thesis. This index will lag behind the awarding of the master's degree by several years. A method must be devised to track the names of graduates by periodically checking for publications using electronic databases.

A *Ph.D. dissertation index* can be calculated and would include the average number of papers published in refereed journals per dissertation. Clearly this index will lag behind the awarding of the Ph.D. degree since it takes time for each individual to get established and then find the time to extract one or more articles from the dissertation research and submit them for publication.

A *conference publication index* is produced by counting the number of referred conference papers accepted and delivered per faculty member per year. In some cases, this index can be refined to reflect the quality of the conference.

It is also possible for a library to create a survey that asks those involved with a research project to indicate the value of the library's physical collections as well as providing access to electronic databases. The value might be in time saved, money saved, new ideas generated, and so forth.

In a large number of studies covering a range of institutional settings, José-Marie Griffiths and Donald King identified the value of apparent information services in the lives of researchers. They focused on the time and effort that would be required by an individual to identify, locate, order, receive, and use the needed information compared to the time required if these tasks were performed by the library. If the library were eliminated and other sources of information were used to provide the equivalent information, the organization would spend considerably more than it does for a library.[22] Granted that Griffith and King studied researchers working in government and private research organizations and that differences exist in an academic environment, yet it is possible to imagine using similar survey techniques to identify the value of the library in the lives of researchers and faculty on campus.

A study at the University of Pittsburgh found that *if* the library's journal collection—physical and electronic—were not available, faculty and researchers would spend an additional 250,000 hours and some $2.1 million to use alternative sources to locate the desired articles.[23] The study used a contingent valuation methodology, which asks survey respondents how much time and money they would spend to obtain the information they currently receive from the library's journal collection if the library collection were unavailable. Further analysis suggested that the net value of the library's journal collection to the university was $11.61 million. Thus, if there were no university library journal collection, it would cost the university 4.38 times the cost of the current library collection in faculty time and other expenditures for the same amount of research and information gathering to be carried out.

By providing timely, quality information services that meet the needs of the professional researchers and faculty, it is hoped that the library helps to increase the quality, timeliness, and productivity of these individuals and ultimately enhances the performance of the university.

Faculty and researchers spend a considerable amount of time reading journal articles, books, research reports, and other documents (professionals average 198 readings per year), according to Griffiths and King. These professionals report spending a lot of time reading—an average of 288 hours per year—which is necessary for them to perform their work and to stay current in their field. This reading, in turn, leads these individuals to avoid having to do certain work, modify their existing work, or stopping an unproductive line of work. These same professionals estimated the value of receiving information from the library—as opposed to their acquiring the documents themselves. On average, the return on investment ranged from 7.8 to 1 to 14.2 to 1.

Summary

Clearly the assessment of the library's contribution to the research environment has not been high on anyone's radar screen, as evidenced by the dearth of research in this area. The approaches used to date have been fairly straightforward but have not addressed the issue of how the library positively influences the quantity and quality of research that is accomplished on campus.

The cost-benefit study that focused on the value of the library-provided print and electronic journals prepared at the University of Pittsburgh is one encouraging project that should be replicated in other institutions. And other creative projects should be tested in an attempt to better understand the value of the academic library to the institution's research community.

Notes

1. J. P. Rushton, and S. Meltzer. Research Productivity, University Revenue, and Scholarly Impact (Citations) of 169 British, Canadian, and United States Universities. *Scientometrics*, 3, 1981, 275–303.

2. John M. Budd. Faculty Publishing Productivity: An Institutional Analysis and Comparison with Library and Other Measures. *College & Research Libraries*, 56 (6), November 1995, 547–54; and John M. Budd. Increases in Faculty Publishing Activity: An Analysis of ARL and ACRL Institutions. *College & Research Libraries*, 60, 1999, 308–15.

3. James C. Baughman and Martha E. Kieltyka. Farewell to Alexandria: Not Yet! *Library Journal*, 124 (5), 1999, 48–49.

4. Christopher Orpen. The Effect of Managerial Distribution of Scientific and Technical Information on Company Performance. *R&D Management*, 15 (4), October 1985, 305–8.

5. Joel D. Goldhar, Louis K. Bragaw, and Jules J. Schwartz. Information Flows, Management Styles, and Technological Innovation. *IEEE Transactions on Engineering Management*, 23 (1), February 1987, 51–61.

6. Michael E. Koenig. The Information and Library Environment and the Productivity of Research. *Inspel*, 24 (4), 1990, 157–67; Michael E. Koenig. Bibliometric Indicators Versus Expert Opinion in Accessing Research Performance. *Journal of the American Society for Information Science*, 34 (2), March 1983, 136–45; Michael E. Koenig. A Bibliometric Analysis of the Pharmaceutical Research. *Research Policy,* 12 (1), February 1983, 15–36.

7. Rosabeth M. Kanter. *The Change Masters: Innovations for Productivity in the American Corporation.* New York: Simon & Schuster, 1983.

8. James M. Utterback. The Process of Technological Innovation Within the Firm. *Academy of Management Journal*, 14, March 1971, 75–88.

9. Mariam Ginman. Information Culture and Business Performance. *IATUL Quarterly,* 2 (2), 1988, 93–106.

10. G. K. Zipf. *Human Behavior and the Principle of Least Effort.* Cambridge, MA: Addison-Wesley, 1949.

11. Victor Resenberg. Factors Affecting the Preferences of Industrial Personnel for Information Gathering Methods. *Information Storage and Retrieval,* 3, 1967, 119–27.

12. Shaun Briley. Innovation and Information: Researchers Cite Increasingly Important Link. *Library Connect,* 4 (1), January 2006, 3.

13. Brinley Franklin. Academic Research Library Support of Sponsored Research in the United States. *Proceedings of the 4th Northumbria International Conference on Performance Measurement in Libraries and Information Services.* Pittsburgh, Pennsylvania, August 12 to 16, 2001, 105–11.

14. Sarah M. Pritchard. Determining Quality in Academic Libraries. *Library Trends,* 44, 1996, 572–94; and Bonnie G. Lindauer. Defining and Measuring the Library's Impact on Campuswide Outcomes. *College & Research Libraries,* 59 (6), 1998, 546–70.

15. J. S. Fairweather. The Highly Productive Faculty Member: Confronting the Mythologies of Faculty Work, in W. G. Tierney, ed., *Faculty Productivity: Facts, Fictions, and Issues.* New York: Falmer Press, 1999, 55–98.

16. Halil Dunbar and Darrell R. Lewis. Determinants of Research Productivity in Higher Education. *Research in Higher Education,* 39 (6), 1998, 607–31.

17. For more information, visit http://www.arl.org/stats/newmeas/mines.html (accessed March 22, 2007).

18. Brinley Franklin and Terry Plum. Networked Electronic Services Usage Patterns at Four Academic Health Sciences Libraries. *Performance Measurement & Metrics,* 3 (3), 2002, 123–33. Available at www.arl.org/stats/newmeas/emetrics/Franklin_081102.pdf (accessed March 22, 2007).

19. Brinley Franklin and Terry Plum. Library Usage Patterns in the Electronic Information Environment. *Information Research,* 9 (4), July 2004, paper 187. Available at http://InformationR.net/ir/9-4/paper187.html (accessed March 22, 2007).

20. Franklin, Academic Research Library Support of Sponsored Research in the United States, 105–11.

21. Bruce Heterick and Roger C. Schonfeld. The Future Ain't What It Used to Be. *Serials*, 17 (3), November 2004, 225–30.

22. José-Marie Griffiths and Donald W. King. *Special Libraries: Increasing the Information Edge*. Washington, DC: Special Libraries Association, 1993.

23. Donald W. King, Sarah Aerni, Fern Brody, Matt Hebison, and Amy Knapp. *The Use and Outcomes of University Library Print and Electronic Collections*. Pittsburgh: University of Pittsburgh, Sara Fine Institute for Interpersonal Behavior and Technology, April 2004; and Donald W. King, Sarah Aerni, Fern Brody, Matt Hebison, and Paul Kohberger. *Comparative Cost of the University of Pittsburgh Electronic and Print Library Collections*. Pittsburgh: University of Pittsburgh, Sara Fine Institute for Interpersonal Behavior and Technology, May 2004. See also Roger C. Schonfeld, Donald W. King, Ann Okerson, and Eileen Gifford Fenton. Library Periodicals Expenses: Comparison of Non-Subscription Costs of Print and Electronic Formats on a Life-Cycle Basis. *D-Lib Magazine*, 10 (1), January 2004. Available at http://www.dlib.org/dlib/january04/schonfeld/01schonfeld.html (accessed March 22, 2007); and Donald W. King, Carol Tenopir, Carol Hansen Montgomery, and Sarah E. Aerni. Patterns of Journal Use by Faculty at Three Diverse Universities. *D-Lib Magazine*, 9 (10), October 2003. http://www.dlib.org/dlib/october03/king/10king.html (accessed March 22, 2007).

Chapter

8

Development of a Library Assessment Plan

*One challenge associated with creating a culture of
assessment in libraries relates to professional values. A profession that inherently believes that it is a
"pubic good" does not feel the need to demonstrate
outcomes and articulate impact. There is a deeply
held and tacit assumption that the "good" is widely
recognized and that the value of library service is
universally appreciated. In the current environment
of competition and of questioning every assumption,
this deeply held value results in resistance to change
and resistance to continuous improvement.*—Amos
Lakos and Shelley Phipps.[1]

The development of a library assessment plan requires a substantial commitment on the part of the library director. The director must provide strong
leadership since assessment will require resources—money for staff to be re-
leased from their regular duties, money for surveys and other data collection efforts, and so forth. Even if the staff are excited about assessment, it will be
difficult, if not impossible, to develop an assessment plan and see it through to
fruition without the wholehearted support of the director and other top
administrative staff:

> Organizations that improve do so because they create and nurture
> agreement on what is worth achieving, and they set in motion the
> internal processes by which people progressively learn how to do
> what they need to do in order to achieve what is worthwhile.[2]

Ten years ago, Peter Hernon and Ellen Altman suggested that an academic library should annually publish the following measures as a reflection of the library's contribution toward teaching and research.[3] Hernon and Altman indicated that they were unaware of any academic library that had ever published such data.

- The percentage of courses using the reserve reading room
- The percentage of students enrolled in those courses who actually checked out reserve materials
- The percentage of courses requiring term papers based on materials from the library
- The number of students who checked out library materials
- The percentage of faculty who checked out library materials
- The percentage of courses using reading packets based on materials photocopied from the library's collection
- The number of articles and books published by faculty members
- The number of references cited in faculty publications from materials contained in the collection

Another six measures were suggested by Karen Bottrill and Victor Borden:

- Percentage of courses requiring students to use the library for research projects
- Number of items checked out of the library by undergraduates
- Number of library computer searches initiated by undergraduates
- Percentage of library study spaces occupied by students
- Number of pages photocopied by students
- Percentage of freshmen students not checking out a library book[4]

Clearly the majority of these measures are output measures, but the intent is to begin to understand the impact of the library in the lives of students, faculty, and researchers.

When considering the prospect of developing an assessment plan for an academic library, the challenge will at times seem daunting and almost Herculean. Yet upon reflection, it is possible to break down the process into manageable stages, as illustrated in Figure 8.1.

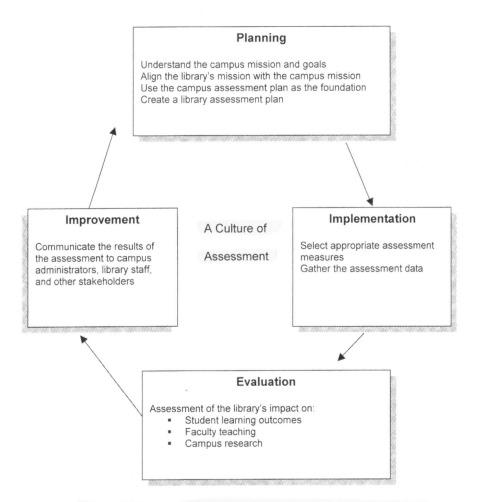

Figure 8.1. Planning and Implementation of a Library Assessment Plan

Planning

Planning for the creation and implementation of a library assessment plan involves several activities, including

- understanding the campus mission and goals,
- aligning the library's mission with the campus mission,
- using the campus assessment plan as the foundation, and
- creating the plan.

Understanding the Campus Mission and Goals

The value of a clear and understandable mission statement for any organization has been articulated by many and was summarized in an earlier chapter of this book. In addition, the accreditation commissions have underscored the importance of the mission statement since they use it as the foundation for their periodic accreditation visits. Thus the college's mission statement forms the backdrop for the library to refine or improve its own mission statement. Refer to chapter 2 for more about mission statements.

In addition, the library's assessment plan must acknowledge and anticipate the perceptions of the library's effectiveness held by the various constituencies, both on campus and the university's board and/or the state. Directing a conversation with these stakeholders to the topic of what is their view of what constitutes a "good" library will be both revealing and helpful. These different perceptions of effectiveness must then become a component of the library's assessment plan. As Bruce Fraser et al. note:

> It is particularly important to distinguish between outcomes of interest, desired outcomes, and actual outcomes. Among the myriad if not infinite outcomes of the research university enterprise . . . *outcomes of interest*—relatively few in number—on which a particular university chooses to focus its attention at a given time, taking into account the complex, ever-changing array of relevant, local values. Of great significance, these outcomes must not only be important to the university's leadership and constituency, but they must also be ones the university determines it can affect *and* measure meaningfully.[5]

Aligning the Library's Mission with the Campus Mission

Consider your library's existing mission statement and determine whether it is aligned with the university's mission statement. Are the mission statements compatible, and does the library's mission statement reflect goals that will assist the university in meeting its mission and goals?[6] If the primary focus of the university is on teaching, then the library's mission should be focused on activities that assist faculty in improving the content of their courses and determining what activities and services will have the greatest impact on improving student achievement. Similarly, if the focus is on research, then the library needs to determine what services are valued and have an impact on the faculty and researchers affiliated with the university.

If needed, the library should revise its mission statement so that it is more closely aligned with the parent institution's mission. Involving the library's stakeholders in the process of revising the mission statement will ensure that the end result is acceptable.

Using the Campus Assessment Plan as the Foundation

> *Most college campuses are awash in data but thirsty for information.*
> —Daniel Seymour[7]

Understanding the educational institution's assessment plan will afford the library the opportunity of potentially piggybacking on some data collection activities. Since an excellent assessment plan will use a variety of methods and measures to determine the extent of student learning or the impact on research activities, there may be opportunities for the library to expand an existing campus survey or other data collection effort as a means of helping to understand the impact of the library on the students, faculty members, and researchers.

The more widespread the educational institution's assessment plan and the extent to which assessment activities have been integrated into courses and programmatic assessments, the more opportunities there will be for the library to lower its data collection costs and create a complementary assessment plan.

The team involved in creating the library's assessment plan should review and discuss the list of questions developed by Bruce Fraser, Charles McClure, and Emily Leahy (see the appendix). It is also helpful to meet with other units on campus to gain a better understanding of the existing assessment efforts on campus.

Creating the Library Assessment Plan

Most library assessment plans will include the usual types of input, process, and output performance measures. However, a comprehensive library assessment plan might have two major outcomes-based assessment efforts: assessment of student learning and assessment of the library's contribution to research. A variety of assessment methods will need to be employed, and some of the methods should be used on a consistent basis so that longitudinal time line data can be created. Some of the assessment methods that might be used are identified and discussed here. Any plan should be focused on assessing *progress,* since the goal of assessment is to improve rather than to demonstrate that the library has arrived at its final destination.

The value of the assessment plan is that it will help campus administrators to see libraries not merely as ends in themselves (self-contained units) but as strategic tools that can be used to achieve goals and objectives. Historically libraries have reported input, process, and output measures, but increasingly the library is being asked to develop outcome measures.

It may be helpful to develop a list of surveys and other data collection efforts that the library already routinely participates in.

Three questions can be used to determine the specifics of what is meant by assessment, direct the methods that should be used, and guide the utilization of the results:[8]

- What is the *purpose* of assessment? Why is it taking place?
    - Enhancement of teaching and learning or *formative* assessment?
    - Accountability to external organizations or *summative* assessment?
- What is the *level* of assessment? Who is to be assessed?
    - Individual students?
    - Groups—aggregation by course, department, college, gender, users versus nonusers of the library, and so forth?
- What *outcomes* are to be assessed?
    - Skills?
    - Knowledge?
    - Attitudes?
    - Behaviors?

Should the library formulate "if . . . then" hypotheses as a part of the assessment planning process, the result will likely be outcomes measures that will be able to answer such questions as the following:

- Will the academic performance of students be improved through the use of the library's resources and services? Assessment will require identifying changes that occurred as the result of service delivery or gaining access to library resources. This will likely require a within-group design (a before versus after analysis) or a between-group design (use of the library group compared to nonuse of the library control group.
- Are undergraduate library users more likely to do better in graduate school?
- Do students who use the library improve the probability that they will have a successful career?
- Does the library's information literacy instruction program improve the student's academic success?
- Will faculty report use of the library's resources improving their teaching or research?

If the library is interested in considering the use of outcomes as part of its assessment plan, then the generic outcomes shown in Table 8.1 should be of interest. These outcomes, which are not meant to be an exhaustive list, provide the

Table 8.1 Generic Outcomes*

Knowledge and Understanding	Knowing about something Learning facts/information Making sense of something Learning how libraries operate Giving specific information: naming things, people, or places Making links and relationships between things Using prior knowledge in new ways
Skills	Knowing how to do something Being able to do new things Intellectual skills: reading, thinking critically and analytically, making judgments Key skills: numbers and statistics, literacy, use of IT, learning how to learn Information management skills: finding, assessing, and using Social skills Communication skills
Attitudes and Values	Feelings Perceptions Opinions about selves, e.g., self-esteem Opinions or attitudes about other people Increased capacity for tolerance Empathy Increased motivation Attitudes toward the library Positive and negative attitudes in relation to experience
Enjoyment, Inspiration, and Creativity	Having fun Being surprised Innovative thoughts Creativity Exploration and experimentation Being inspired
Activity, Behavior, and Progression	What people do What people intend to do (intention to act) What people have done A change in the way people manage their time Reported or observed actions

*Adapted from Jennifer Cram and Valerie Shine. Performance Measurement as Promotion: Demonstrating Benefit to Your Significant Others. Paper presented at the School Library Association of Queensland Biennial Conference, 29 June–1 July 2004, Gold Coast, Queensland. Available at http://www.alia.org.au/~jcram/ PMasPromotion.pdf (accessed March 22, 2007).

library with a framework for assessing the impact of the library on students, faculty, and researchers. These outcomes can assist the library in beginning to frame the discussion with others on campus about learning and how the library contributes in both formal and informal ways.

Implementation

Implementation of the library's assessment plan involves selecting appropriate assessment measures and gathering and analyzing the assessment data.

Selecting Appropriate Assessment Measures

The assessment plan should reflect the fact that some data will be collected periodically, e.g., every two to three years, while other data will be collected much more frequently. The assessment plan should be phased so as to not overwhelm library staff members. It is important to recognize that assessment works best when it is ongoing, not episodic.

A portion of the library's assessment plan might include a comparison to a set of measures reflecting the performance of peer libraries. The vast majority of libraries have been using such comparisons for some time. As such, a library will typically compare itself to peer libraries using input or resource measures, process or productivity measures, and output measures.[9] However, these comparisons should occupy only a small portion of the library's assessment plan. The plan must take a broader perspective and focus on outcomes! Outcomes are the ways in which students and faculty are changed as a result of their contact with the library's resources and services.

> *Academic libraries should develop a process to identify and to operationalize library outcomes that contribute to institutional outcomes. The library must play a major role in informing the university of valued institutional outcomes to which the library contributes. Setting up such a process is an important method for informing key stakeholders in the university of both the library's role in institutional outcomes and ensuring that the institutional outcomes to which the library has (or may have) links are appropriate.*
> —Bruce Fraser, Charles McClure, and Emily Leahy[10]

The library might include measures such as inclusion in course syllabi and integration of library use into the undergraduate curriculum, but these are process measures that indicate the activities the library is undertaking to encourage use of the library.

Unfortunately the *Standards for Libraries in Higher Education*, adopted by the ACRL Board of Directors in June 2004, provides little guidance and encouragement to move to outcome measures.[11] This eight-page document details input and output measures and addresses such topics as instruction, planning, resources, access, and staff. Yet it only asks one question about outcomes "What outcomes does the library measure, and how does it measure these outcomes?"

The characteristics of a good assessment plan include positive answers to the following:

- Are student learning goals identified?

- Will the library's contribution to helping students achieve their goals be addressed by the assessment procedure?

- Are multiple assessment measures used?

- Are the measures understood and valued by all stakeholders?

- Does the plan identify the people (committees) involved and the processes that will be used?

- Are the results of assessment having an impact on the planning process so that changes are made to improve the impact of the library on students, faculty, and researchers? Stakeholders understand that an assessment plan for the institution as well as for academic departments and support units such as the library naturally evolves and matures over time. Recognizing this fact, the North Central Association of Colleges and Schools developed a "Levels of Implementation" matrix that has three levels: beginning implementation of assessment programs, making progress in implementing assessment programs, and maturing stages of continuous improvement.[12]

The Library's Contribution to Student Learning

Clearly there is a need to demonstrate that students can *find* appropriate resources and are *satisfied* with the library's collections and services. However, academic libraries need to start assessment activities that will demonstrate that students are improving their *learning* as a result of using the library's resources. This will likely mean that the library will need to identify a set of desired proficiencies and then identify a set of variables that, directly or indirectly, influence impact or effectiveness.

The library should consider assessment of the library's physical collection, electronic resources, information literacy activities, reference services, document delivery/interlibrary loan services, building (space for studying and providing access to computer resources), and any other service provided by the library that it feels is important. These assessment efforts should be using the students' work—be they undergraduate or graduate students—as the focal point.

Depending on the type of assessment activity, it may be necessary for the library to obtain the approval of an Institutional Review Board to protect the privacy and rights of human research subjects.

The Library's Collections

The library is the embalming of dead genius.—
John Henry Newman [13]

Several older studies examined the use of the library's physical collections and student achievement as evidenced by better grades, better research papers (which should lead to better grades), student retention rates, time to graduate, and graduation rates.[14] The preparation of such studies required only a moderate amount of resources. Historically, libraries have prepared evaluations that determined the accessibility of the collections: Were students, faculty, and researchers finding what they were looking for? Such evaluations are internally focused and are only an indirect measure of the possible use of the collections.

In the past, the assumption was made that, all other things being equal, a service will be more beneficial the more it is used by the library's customers. In other words, if the customer was borrowing materials, visiting the library (physically or electronically), asking reference questions, and so forth, the library must be doing a good job. Yet reporting input and output measures—which answer questions such as "How many?" and "How much?"—adds little analysis and insight of the library's worth to the customer! If the contribution of the library cannot be deduced from the size of its collections, number of circulation transactions, number of reference queries, and use of the library's Web site, by what measures will a library know that it is meeting the needs of students and scholars?

Measures designed to show the impact or effect a library's resources and services have on individuals and the cumulative impact on the institution as a whole are know as outcome measures. Outcome measures reflect changes in an individual's behavior, skills, knowledge, perceptions, or attitudes. Thus, outcome measures are focusing on effectiveness and answer such questions as "How well?" and "How valuable?"

If the physical collection no longer defines the library, then the role of the library will be called into question by some. The library must strengthen its relationship to the mission of the university and have its contributions measured and assessed. The challenge for a library is significant, and it must be addressed soon.

Electronic Resources

As spending by an academic library continues to increase for electronic resources, the library is faced with the need to measure the scope and value of providing access to digital collections.

A recent large-scale survey conducted by OCLC pointed to the fact that 89 percent of college students use search engines to begin an information search and only 2 percent begin their searching using a library Web site. College students use the library less and read less since they started using the Internet, and when they do visit the library it is as a place to do homework and study. It is also significant that the library brand among students is "books." This means that the other services offered by libraries are often not considered by students as being relevant.[15]

David Lewis suggests that academic librarians should not be surprised by the OCLC findings. He notes:

> As a general rule, library managers have no idea how much time it takes to use their libraries. If they were to estimate the time requirements, they would find that they significantly underestimate how much time is actually required for library use. This leads to the situation where libraries think they are charging less than they actually are, and they are unprepared when quicker ways of getting information emerge and take away many of their customers.[16]

Recently, the MINES for Libraries project developed a Web-based survey that asks how students, professors, and researchers are using the electronic resources provided by the library—funded research, non-funded research, instruction/education, student research papers, and course work.[17] The library might replicate or use this tool as a start for assessment efforts in this area. It might extend this survey by asking the respondent to rate the utility of the electronic resources. Since the respondent is asked to complete the survey before being allowed to proceed to with the search, some view this as intrusive.

Some libraries have used Web analysis software (sometimes transaction log analysis) to determine where and what kind of use is being made of electronic resources when the user is either in the library or on campus. While providing some helpful information, this approach does not reveal anything about distant users and their searching behaviors.

The vendors of electronic resources are moving, albeit slowly, to provide a standardized set of statistics (Project COUNTER) about the use of their databases for their customer libraries.

Other assessment methodologies that might be used are interviews and surveys of customer preferences, interviews and surveys of behavioral questions, focus groups, and observations.

Information Literacy Activities

The majority of evaluation efforts in the area of information literacy have focused on student satisfaction and/or abilities that have been developed as a result of a either a library-provided class or the integration of information literacy into other course content—typically using a pre-test and post-test methodology. As noted in chapter 5, the studies assessing both student satisfaction and developing information literacy skills are decidedly mixed and paint a fairly bleak picture. The Web-based Project SAILS survey instrument can be used to assess the increased information literacy skills as the result of instruction—directly by library-taught classes or indirectly by integrating information literacy skills into the curriculum.[18]

Information literacy assessment efforts that link information literacy skills with better overall grades, higher retention rates, and so forth are clearly needed. In such cases, the use of a control group (a group of similar students who do not receive the information literacy training) will lead to more credible results.

Reference Services

The majority of evaluation efforts in the area of reference have been internally focused. That is, libraries have examined a variety of aspects pertaining to reference such as queuing times, service times, hours and cost of service, and so forth as well as providing training to improve the reference interview and customer interactions. By design, such evaluation efforts clearly help to improve the quality of service in an individual library but do not help the library understand the bigger picture—how reference impacts students and faculty members.

The choice of an assessment methodology for reference services is further complicated since these services are increasingly being done electronically—through instant messaging, e-mail, fax, and 24/7 chat—as well as through the more traditional in-person and telephone services.

Libraries that have evaluated the quality of their reference services have, for the most part, focused on the customer service aspects of providing this service. An academic library might employ a similar approach to that used by the MINES for Libraries project in asking reference service customers to indicate the primary reason for using the service as well as the value or utility of the service. Reference services will have an immediate short-term outcome: improving the quality of information being accessed, reducing the time spent in acquiring the information, or improving the quality of a research proposal or report, among many possible outcomes. Whether the use of reference services has long-term outcomes for students and faculty will need to be established (most likely using a longitudinal research design).

Another possibility would be to send an e-mail following a reference contact, with the obvious approval of the library customer, to determine the reason for the contact as well as soliciting an indication of the value or utility of the information provided.

Assessment of Document Delivery/Interlibrary Loan Services

A great many academic libraries have seen an increase in the use of document delivery and interlibrary loan services. It would be possible to ask the recipients of such services how they use the materials that are provided to them: preparation of a term paper, research report, master's thesis or Ph.D. dissertation, and so forth. The recipients could also be queried about their perceptions of the value, to them, of these services.

It would also be possible to determine the frequency with which the supplied materials are used and cited in the research report, dissertation, or term paper. However, it is important to note that while some items may not be cited, they could potentially have a positive impact on the student, faculty member, or researcher.

Assessment of the Library Building

An analysis of the library building's use and activity levels may reveal that changes need to be made to better meet the needs of students and faculty. Additional group study spaces and technology workstations may be needed as well as providing such amenities as a coffee bar and opportunities for social interactions.

The library may wish to survey its users as well as conduct focus groups with students who do not use the library.

The Library's Contribution to Institutional Research

To establish the value of the library to the institution's research efforts, the library will need to ask those involved in research and using the library's resources and services to indicate the extent of their use and provide an indication of the value of such use. Such an assessment effort might involve a survey that asks the respondent to rate the utility of the information received from the library. The survey might take several forms, and the form should be selected after consulting with a number of researchers (perhaps using a focus group as a means to gain insights).

The library may also be a partner in a research proposal submitted for funding. As such, the library's contribution should be communicated to the campus administrators.

Select Appropriate Assessment Measures

Once the library has identified what area(s) it wishes to start to use as a focal point for the creation of a library assessment plan, it should carefully consider the possible ways in which to collect data. The strengths and limitations of each approach should be weighed and then an assessment method should be selected.

It is helpful to complete the form shown in Table 8.2, which identifies the assessment outcome, the indicator or performance measure that will be used, the source of the data, and how frequently the data will be gathered and analyzed. A sample of the outcome logic model for several perspectives is also provided in Table 8.3.

Table 8.2 Outcome Logic Model

Outcome	Indicator	Applied To	Source of Data	Data Collection Interval

Gathering and Analyzing the Assessment Data

Determine who will be responsible for collecting and analyzing the data. And while it may be prudent to assign responsibility for different surveys and data collection activities to different people, ultimately these individuals should report back to the library director or assistant director who has been charged with assessment responsibilities. The assessment plan therefore incorporates the need for management time and resources to ensure that the projects are successfully completed.

One important caveat is that the different steps in the assessment plan and data collection and analysis process will require different skills. Poorly trained researchers can jeopardize the evaluation effort, as noted by Denise Troll Covey.[19] Thus, a library will need to invest in its staff members acquiring a variety of skills in order for assessment to produce positive results. The library's assessment plan and the selection of performance measures will determine the mix of skills that will be needed. Remember that in most cases, other assessment-related skills can be tapped from other campus departments.

Table 8.3 Outcome Logic Model Samples

Outcome	Indicator	Applied To	Source of Data	Data Collection Interval
Students who complete a course with an integrated information literacy component or complete a library-provided information literacy course and earn higher grades than their peers	Number/percent of students who earn better grades than their peers—use of a control group of students with similar SAT scores, socioeconomic backgrounds, and so forth	Undergraduate students	Analysis of transcripts	Annually
Students who use interlibrary loan/document delivery and use the materials in term papers, theses, and dissertations and report that their resulting work has been improved	Number/percent of ILL/DD materials used (cited) in term papers, theses, and dissertations	Undergraduate and graduate students	Survey of undergraduate and graduate students. Random sample selected from all who used the service in the last six months	Every six months
Faculty who use interlibrary loan/document delivery and use the materials in improving the content of a course	Number/percent of ILL/DD materials used by the faculty member and reported to be of value	Faculty	Survey of faculty	Annually
Students who use library-provided electronic resources (databases) and use the materials in term papers, theses, and dissertations and report that their resulting work has been improved	Number/percent of electronic resources materials (articles downloaded) used (cited) in term papers, theses, and dissertations	Undergraduate and graduate students	Survey of undergraduate and graduate students. Random sample selected from all who used the service in the last six months	Every six months

Table 8.3 Outcome Logic Model Samples (*Continued*)

Outcome	Indicator	Applied To	Source of Data	Data Collection Interval
Faculty who use library-provided electronic resources (databases) and use the downloaded materials in a published article or research report	Number/percent of electronic articles downloaded used by the faculty member and reported to be of value	Faculty	Survey of faculty Alternatively: Track what citations were used in published articles, conference presentations, and books by the faculty.	Annually
Students who borrow materials from the library's physical collection and do better academically than their counterparts who do not borrow materials	Number/percent of students who earn better grades than their peers—use of a control group of students with similar SAT scores, socioeconomic backgrounds, and so forth	Undergraduate students	Analysis of transcripts and circulation data	Annually
Faculty who borrow materials from the library's physical collection and report that it helped them improve the content of a course	Number/percent of faculty that report the borrowed materials assisted them in improving the content of a course they are teaching	Faculty	Survey of faculty and circulation data	Annually
Faculty who borrow materials from the library's physical collection and report that they included citations to the material in articles or books they have authored or conference presentations they have made	Number/percent of faculty that report the borrowed materials assisted them in improving the articles/books they are writing or a conference presentation they have made	Faculty	Survey of faculty and circulation data	Annually

Evaluation

Once the data have been collected and analyzed, the library should prepare a report that presents the plan, data collection efforts, a presentation and analysis of the data, and a set of conclusions and recommendations. With the report in hand, the library should take the time to reflect on the results. Among the questions that should be asked are the following:

- Does the data collection method accurately reflect the outcomes?
- Are there a sufficient number of responses to ensure that the resulting statistical analysis will be robust?
- Do the complementary assessment methods chosen by the library tell a similar story?

Improvement

The results of the analysis should be written up in a report so that it can be shared with library staff members, campus administrators, and other interested stakeholders. The results of the library's assessment plan, which will contain several complementary outcome measures, can be combined with data comparing and contrasting your library with your peer libraries (which libraries have historically done). For the most part, this comparison with peer libraries will utilize input, process, and outcome measures.

Prepare for the Next Time

Remember that assessment is a process and not a goal. The goal is to improve the quality and relevance of library services to students, faculty, researchers, and campus administrators. As such assessment is not a one-shot event but an ongoing process. After the library has published the results of its first library assessment plan and received feedback and comments from a variety of stakeholders, reflect on how the library can make the assessment plan better. But most important, act on the information garnered as the result of the assessment efforts.

Thought-Provoking Questions*

- **Will the evidence provided by the assessment method be linked to important student learning outcomes?** Regardless of the assessment methods or evaluation tools selected, it is important to ensure that the data being gathered will provide evidence of the desired learning outcomes. It is important to verify the validity of the instrument being used to collect the data. Even use of a national standardized test still needs to be reviewed to ensure that what is being tested will accurately reflect what is being taught.

- **Is the evaluation method comprehensive?** No assessment tool or evaluation method can assess every important learning outcome, but the best ones assess a representative sample of important learning outcomes. And while it is probably not financially feasible to subject students to multiple tests or surveys, it is still important to have more than one method of assessment. One important selection criterion for any assessment is how comprehensive the test or survey is.

- **Are important learning outcomes evaluated by multiple means?** Assessing important learning goals through a variety of means and formats is important since no evaluation method is perfect. While a standardized test of disciplinary knowledge may be an adequate form of assessment of students' content knowledge, it will not provide an indication of the student's preparedness to be a good practitioner in a particular discipline.

- **Are the responses interpreted in the same way?** When assessments employ a subjective evaluation method, it is important to have created a scoring rubric (criteria used to score or rate responses) to ensure comparability of review. Clearly an agreement needs to be reached as to what constitutes inadequate, acceptable, and exemplary responses or performance. Utilizing two or more colleagues to "grade" each student's work will improve inter-rater reliability.

- **Do the results make sense?** When developing an assessment plan, interpreting data resulting from assessment instruments, and so forth, it is important to ensure that a dose of common sense is employed. The expected should not be surprising, while the unexpected should trigger further inquiries. After all, the purpose of assessment and analysis is insight!

> • **Are the results corroborated by other evidence?** The results
> of assessment are always improved when multiple means of as-
> sessment are used. The methods might be quantitative and quali-
> tative, direct and indirect. For example, do students who perform
> well in an assessment of writing skills also have good grades in
> composition classes? Focus groups should complement survey
> results. Do faculty ratings and student self-assessment ratings
> parallel one another?
>
> *These questions are adapted from the Middle States Commission on Higher Educa-
> tion. *Student Learning Assessment: Options and Resources*. Philadelphia: The Middle
> States Commission on Higher Education, 2003.

Notes

1. Amos Lakos and Shelley Phipps. Crating a Culture of Assessment: A Catalyst for Organizational Change. *portal: Libraries and the Academy*, 4 (3), July 2004, 345–61.

2. Michael Fullan. *Leading in a Culture of Change*. San Francisco: Jossey-Bass, 2001, 125.

3. Peter Hernon and Ellen Altman. *Service Quality in Academic Libraries*. Norwood, NJ: Ablex Publishing, 1996, 1–2.

4. Karen V. Bottrill and Victor M. H. Borden. Appendix. Examples from the Literature, in Victor M. H. Borden and Trudy W. Banta, eds., *Using Performance Indicators to Guide Strategic Decision Making*. San Francisco: Jossey-Bass, 1994, 107–19.

5. Bruce T. Fraser, Charles R. McClure, and Emily H. Leahy. Toward a Framework for Assessing Library and Institutional Outcomes. *portal: Libraries and the Academy*, 2 (4), 2002, 505–28.

6. For more about strategic planning and mission and vision statements, see Joseph R. Matthews. *Strategic Planning and Management for Library Managers*. Westport, CT: Libraries Unlimited, 2005.

7. Daniel Seymour. *Once Upon a Campus: Lessons for Improving Quality and Productivity in Higher Education*. Phoenix, AZ: Oryx, 1995, 80.

8. P T. Terenzini. Assessment with Open Eyes: Pitfalls in Studying Student Outcomes. *Journal of Higher Education*, 60, 1989, 644–64.

9. The library may wish to create a set of comparisons following the structure suggested by William Neal Nelson and Robert W. Fernekes in *Standard and Assessment for Academic Libraries: A Workbook.* Chicago: ACRL, 2002.

10. Fraser, McClure, and Leahy. Toward a Framework for Assessing Library and Institutional Outcomes, 523.

11. The standard is available at www.ala.org/ala/acrl/acrlstandards/ standardslibraries.htm (accessed March 22, 2007).

12. *Assessment of Student Academic Achievement: Levels of Implementation. Addendum to the Handbook of Accreditation.* 2d ed. Chicago: The Higher Leaning Commission of the North Central Association of Colleges and Schools, 2002.

13. John Henry Newman. Rise and Progress of Universities, in *Essays and Sketches.* New York: Longmans, 1948, 328.

14. See, for example, W. E. Troutt. Regional Accreditation Evaluation Criteria and Quality Assurance. *Journal of Higher Education*, 50 (2), 1979, 199–210; R. Nichols. Effects of Various College Characteristics on Student Aptitude Test Scores. *Journal of Educational Psychology*, 55 (1), 1964, 45–54; Alexander Astin. Undergraduates Achievement and Institutional "Excellence." *Science*, 161, 1968, 661–68; and D. A. Rock, J. A. Centra, and R. L. Linn. Relationship Between College Characteristics and Student Achievement. *American Educational Research Journal*, 7, 1970, 109–21.

15. Cathy De Rosa, Joanne Cantrell, Janet Hawk, and Alane Wilson. *College Students' Perceptions of Libraries and Information Resources: A Report to the OCLC Membership.* Dublin, OH: OCLC, 2006.

16. David W. Lewis. The Innovator's Dilemma: Disruptive Change and Academic Libraries. *Library Administration & Management*, 18 (2), Spring 2004, 68–74.

17. For more information, visit http://www.arl.org/stats/newmeas/ mines.html (accessed March 22, 2007).

18. Lisa G. O'Connor, Carolyn J. Radcliff, and Julie A. Gedeon. Applying Systems Design and Item Response Theory to the Problem of Measuring Information Literacy Skills. *College & Research Libraries*, 63 (6), November 2002, 528–43.

19. Denise Troll Covey. Academic Library Assessment: New Duties and Dilemmas. *New Library World*, 103 (1175/1176), 2002, 156–64.

Appendix:
Outcomes Questions for Practitioners

Bruce T. Fraser, Charles R. McClure, and Emily H. Leahy. Toward a Framework for Assessing Library and Institutional Outcomes. *portal: Libraries and the Academy*, 2 (4), 2002, 524–25.

- Is there a culture of assessment at your university? At your library?
- How does your university articulate its core values?
  - Are these values clear? Defined? Measurable?
  - Are these values clearly articulated in the context of the library?
- Does your university measure itself—its outcomes—in terms of its core values?
  - How?
  - What measures/statistics/indicators does your university routinely collect?
  - How does the analysis of these data reflect the values of the institution?
  - How does your university administration use its outcomes data and analysis to change and improve its operations?
  - How does your university administration use its outcomes data and analysis to articulate need for improvements or changes in the operations of the library?
  - How does your library use university outcomes data and analysis to improve the operations of the library?
- Has the culture of assessment remained constant at your university (and at your library), or has it changed relatively recently?
  - If it has changed, what were the causes of the changes? Does it change often?
  - If it has remained constant, does this reflect rigidity in the thinking of the administration as a whole? Does it reflect helpful stability?
- What does your university expect from the library in terms of contributing to university outcomes?
  - Does the university make these expectations clear?
  - What do they need to know to make them clearer?

- What does your university expect from the library in terms of reporting data?

- How receptive do you believe your university administration is or would be to library reporting based on outcomes assessment?

- Does your library currently focus on campuswide, university-based outcomes?

    – If yes, how does your library determine which outcomes to focus on?

    – How are you linking or matching the data you collect with those outcomes?

    – How do you identify those relationships?

- Does your library collect data on its outcomes (impacts, effects)—and/or on university outcomes—that occur outside the library's domain?

    – If yes, how?

    – If no, is it clear how that could be done at your institution?

    – What obstacles do you know of—or perceive or expect—regarding collecting university outcome data across the campus?

- How do you see the way you assess your library's performance changing in the next few years?

    – Why?

    – How should it change?

- Assuming your library does not already do so, if your library were to measure and report its data in terms of university outcomes, would that affect the way the library is viewed and funded by your university's administration?

    – If yes, how would it change?

    – Why?

    – How difficult would it be to effect that change?

- What are the key activities that your library does to support the research, education, and service goals of your university?

    – What kind of formal or informal data does the library collect that let you know you are supporting these goals?

    – How does this play a part in determining the types of resources and services you offer?

    – How could this play a greater role?

Index

About the Author

Joseph R. Matthews is a consultant specializing in strategic planning, assessment and evaluation of library services, the use of performance measures, and the Library Balanced Scorecard. He is also an instructor at the San Jose State University School of Library and Information Science and lives in Carlsbad, California.